Pathways to Constructivism: A Self-directed Guide for Educators

Canadian Child Care Curriculum Study

Authors:

Ellen Jacobs
Goranka Vukelich
Nina Howe

This research was funded by the Social Development Partnerships program, Human Development Resources Canada. The views expressed are solely those of the researchers and do not represent the official policy of the Department of Human Resources Canada.

Principal Investigators:

Ellen Jacobs
Concordia University, Montreal, Quebec

Nina Howe
Concordia University, Montreal, Quebec

Project Coordinator:

Goranka Vukelich
Concordia University, Montreal, Quebec

Curriculum Trainers:

Monica Lytwyn, Winnipeg, Manitoba
Madalena Coutihno, Montreal, Quebec
Chris Kronick, Halifax, Nova Scotia

Research Assistants:

Montreal: Toni Hakem, Emma McLaren, Crystal James
Winnipeg: Elin Ibrahim, Carrie Timgren
Halifax: Maria Sarria, Jane Green

Curriculum Designers:

Shelley Thompson, Halifax, Nova Scotia
Ruth Strubank, Halifax, Nova Scotia
Cathy Mott, Montreal, Quebec
Jill Fortney, Oakville, Ontario

Table of Contents

Acknowledgements

This manual is the product of a research project about in-service training that was conducted in three cities across Canada: Winnipeg, Montreal, and Halifax. Each city had a team that included a curriculum trainer, and two research assistants all of whom worked with the participating centres in each city. We would like to thank the Winnipeg team that consisted of Monica Lytwyn (Curriculum trainer), Elin Ibrahim (Head researcher) and Carrie Timgren (Research assistant); the Montreal team of Madalena Coutihno (Curriculum trainer), Toni Hakem (Head researcher), Emma McLaren (Research Assistant) and Crystal James (Research assistant) as well as Natalie di Francesco, Tomoko Matsuda, Carrie Novinsky and Amanda Parker; and the Halifax team of Chris Kronick (Curriculum trainer), Maria Sarria (Head researcher), and Jane Green (Research assistant). We thank these individuals for their persistence in visiting the centres and gathering the research data during harsh winter weather conditions. We also want to thank them for their careful handling of the data and their dedication to the project.

We must acknowledge the participants for without their cooperation we would not have been able to learn what we did about in-service training. Thus, we would like to thank all of the centre directors who welcomed us into their midst; the educators who agreed to work with us; the parents who agreed to participate, responded to our questionnaires and allowed their children to participate. To the children we owe an enormous thanks for being so good-humoured and willing to take part in this study.

The curriculum designers for this project were Shelley Thompson and Ruth Strubank of Halifax and Cathy Mott of Montreal. Jill Fortney (Oakville) designed the workshop material. We thank these authors for their willingness to share their knowledge and experience and for their devotion to the project. Their ideas and the documentation they provided gave us invaluable material with which to work.

The coordinator of the project was Goranka Vukelich (Montreal). Her in-depth knowledge of Canadian provincial child care systems, her extraordinary organizational abilities and networking skills, and her extensive understanding of constructivism made the project a success. She worked tirelessly to bring every aspect of the project to a successful completion.

We also thank our copy editor Blossom Thom, and our translator Selma Tischer. Their careful attention to detail and sensitivity to expression helped us make this document come alive in both official languages.

Last, but certainly not least, we wish to thank our families; our life partners Peter Jacobs, Allister Thorne, and Bill Bukowski for their support and encouragement throughout this lengthy study and our children Sidney, Ana and Nick for their patience and understanding when our focus was elsewhere A special thanks to Zoe and Maia for making the elements of constructivism come alive.

Introduction

This manual comes with an invitation to explore new pathways in curriculum design; to some it will feel like a road less traveled, to others it may seem like a familiar route. Whatever the case may be for you, we hope you find the map we have created to be interesting, challenging, and worth the trip. Our manual is the result of a research project conducted in 45 child care centres across Canada. We were interested in helping experienced educators implement current ideas about constructivism into their teaching practices. The outcome of our study was so positive that we were asked to share our information with other educators who might be interested in incorporating a constructivist approach in their classroom. To this end we have designed a manual that addresses educators in a personal manner. There are explanations of special terms and interesting activities included in each section to reinforce concepts as they are introduced. We hope you will find the language used throughout the manual very readable and the activities enjoyable and pertinent.

Constructivism is based upon the concept that learning, to be beneficial, must be relevant and meaningful to the learner. In such a framework, learners are viewed as competent, curious individuals who bring valuable ideas and experiences to the learning situation. Learning is also viewed as a process whereby children acquire knowledge about their physical and social world by active engagement with their environment and by communicating with others.

The principles of constructivism that formed the theoretical base of this manual are:

1. Constructivism is a theory of learning that offers an explanation regarding the nature of knowledge and how human beings learn, which can inform our teaching practices.

2. Learners bring valuable knowledge, understanding, and experiences into every learning situation, which they use as the foundation for further learning.

3. Knowledge and understanding are constructed as the learner becomes actively involved and engaged in the learning process. For young children, in particular, a hands-on approach using familiar, concrete materials is recommended.

4. Relevant learning occurs during experiences and in contexts that are important to the child and via collaboration and communication with others. Communication allows learners to actively initiate, debate, and express ideas.

5. Concepts developed about objects, people, or events are not static and will undoubtedly change as the learner encounters new information through additional experiences and inquiry.

6. Misunderstandings are an important component of the learning situation, because they provide opportunities to explore and discuss concepts.

7. For educators, reflecting upon experiences through the use of journal writing, visual documentation, or discussion can assist you in making knowledge and understanding meaningful for the learner.

8. Learning is a life long process.

To integrate and implement constructivist ideas into your teaching practice, it is important to be an accurate observer of the children in your classroom, to have a significant understanding/knowledge of child development, to be flexible about curriculum design, to be able to document children's activities, and to be willing to take time to reflect upon what you have observed and recorded. Through active engagement in all of these processes you will be able to create a relevant and meaningful learning environment that takes into account children's unique needs and interests. It will provide an opportunity for you, as an educator, to enrich your own experiences in the classroom.

Through your observations of the children's interests, competencies, and learning styles and your careful reflection on these observations, you will be able to build on the children's previously expressed ideas and experiences. In so doing you will be able to help them construct knowledge and understanding about their physical and social world in a way that is meaningful to them. For instance, in one classroom, two young children came to school excited about going to the polling station with their parents on Election Day. They chattered about the process of voting and the educator engaged them in a discussion about the meaning of voting, specifically the process of making thoughtful choices. The whole group contributed their ideas about voting and the educator wondered aloud if they would like to vote about something they do on a daily basis in their classroom. The children decided that they would like to vote about their snack. It took them a few days to get set up for the vote. To do so, one group designed the ballots, another group built a polling station, and a third group created flyers with drawings of the food options. On the third day everyone was ready for the vote and once the ballots were cast, the children counted the ballots and determined that apples were preferred over carrots. They then produced a chart indicating the number of votes for apples and carrots to show their parents the outcome of the vote. On the next day, the children cut up apples for their snack.

By encouraging children to investigate topics in which they have shown an interest and doing so in ways that make sense to them, you will nurture their natural curiosity and tendency to construct knowledge and understanding (through appropriate means). In addition, you can acquire curriculum ideas that can be implemented in other parts of the program, thereby creating an integrated, emergent quality to your curriculum design. In the previous example, the educator extended the voting into both a numeracy and a literacy project (documentation chart on voting outcomes) and an opportunity to promote fine-motor development (cutting up apples). No doubt there are many other ways that the experience could be extended into other areas of the curriculum.

In a constructivist classroom, all of the participants are learners and as such there is an excitement about the learning opportunities that each new day brings. This approach entices everyone to come to the classroom with enthusiasm about learning, a desire to explore new concepts, and an enjoyment in discovery.

This manual provides a framework that will guide you through the process of designing and implementing classroom experiences and learning opportunities for children using a constructivist approach. We have identified five pathways to constructivism–values and beliefs, early childhood curriculum, observation, documentation, and reflection–and have expanded upon each of them in a separate chapter. Each pathway can be thought of as one component that is necessary for implementing a constructivist approach in your classroom. While each has value in itself, which is reflected in our creation of five distinct chapters, you will see that the five pathways are interdependent. There are many places in the manual where you will be encouraged to review information presented in one of the other chapters and to consider how the various routes influence and relate to one another. As you work through the manual, you will find information about constructivism, as well as corresponding exercises that have been designed to assist you in exploring this information and in applying it to your individual setting. We invite you to immerse yourself in experiences guided by the principles of constructivism, reflect upon those experiences, connect them to your values and beliefs, and develop relevant and meaningful learning that will strengthen your skills as an early childhood educator.

Finally, we recognize that many of the ideas about constructivism may be familiar to you, although you may also encounter new ideas in our manual. Of course, these may present new challenges. Sometimes new ideas and new ways of interacting are frustrating at first but, if you work collaboratively with the children, we believe that you will be able to implement some of these ideas, making your classroom an exciting place for learning and discovery. Sharing curriculum planning with the children may be perceived to be a challenge, but if you are willing to take this step, it will be an enriching experience for all. Of course, flexibility, the willingness to listen to children, and a keen understanding of the children's behavior and interests are key factors in the constructivist approach. Employing these factors in your teaching practice will create opportunities for children to think creatively and express their own ideas. As you support their learning, you will encourage children to take initiative and responsibility for their own learning, as well as develop an understanding of the world around them. We hope this will be a life long process for all. We hope you enjoy your journey with the children along the pathways of constructivism!

Values and Beliefs

Your values and beliefs play a significant role in determining your classroom practices. They provide the foundation for a philosophy of teaching that guides your interpretation of child development knowledge, your interpretation of your observations of children, and your classroom decision-making. While values and beliefs are closely related, there are significant differences between the two that are worth noting.

Notes!

Value
A value is a deeply held and enduring view of what we believe to be important and worthwhile. Our personal values shape our beliefs about what is important to pursue, how we treat others, and how we choose to spend our time.

--Paula J. Bloom

Your values can be thought of as a "moral compass" or a "centering mechanism" that guides your actions and decisions, either consciously or subconsciously. Values are developed slowly over time and are influenced by age, gender, family, culture, education, and experience. For a variety of reasons, you may feel more strongly about some values than others. As a result, some values may be stronger than others in influencing your beliefs and classroom decision-making.

Belief
A belief is different from a value. It is our personal conviction that certain things are true or that certain statements are facts.

--Paula J. Bloom

Your beliefs are firmly held, personal opinions about various ideas and concepts. They are your truths, the things you believe in. While they are inspired by values, beliefs can be interpreted in numerous ways, and can motivate various actions, making it possible for different people to have different beliefs shaped by the same value.

It is important for you to distinguish between values and beliefs, because it helps to understand that just stating that you "share values" with someone else might not be enough. It is possible that you may have different definitions and convictions (beliefs) about the value in question.

For example, you and a colleague may both indicate that you value *creativity.* For you, defining that value may mean originality, opportunity for problem solving, and numerous choices throughout the day. As a result of these beliefs regarding creativity, you may find yourself stocking many of the classroom centres with empty boxes, egg cartons, and pieces of cloth; encouraging children to use them in various ways; and allowing for flexibility in the amount of time devoted to scheduled activities from day to day. Whereas, for your colleague, creativity may mean supporting the children's use of art materials brought to an activity time by an educator in an original way. As a result of her beliefs, your colleague may implement art activities that are open-ended and support original creations by the children, but may not allow art activity time to spill over into other parts of the schedule or allow the use of art materials during other parts of the day. Thus, for both of you, the same value of creativity is defined and realized in different ways.

In order to have a fuller understanding of your beliefs and classroom practices, it is important to try to articulate and reflect upon the values that inspire them.

Exploring your values and beliefs

Each of us is a complex arrangement of values and beliefs and it will take considerable time and effort to understand what your values and beliefs are, how they relate to each other, how they inspire your classroom decisions, and how they may be similar and different from the values and beliefs of constructivism. Reflecting upon and becoming more aware of your values and beliefs will help you gain a deeper understanding of your current classroom practices. It will also help you to generate alternative classroom practices that are more aligned with constructivism or reinforce those practices that are already in tune with constructivist principles.

Connecting with and understanding your values and beliefs is a central objective of using this manual. As you work through it, you will notice that you will frequently be encouraged to articulate and reflect upon your values and beliefs. Some things to consider as you prepare for this process include:

1. Observation is an important tool in helping you begin to understand and reflect upon your values and beliefs.

2. Individual values may be different based on experience, education, culture, family upbringing, etc., but most groups of people (e.g., educators) have some values in common.

3. Your values are reflected in your work as an educator in the classroom, your relationships with the children and your colleagues, and your daily activities.

4. Discussions of your values and beliefs with others may facilitate your ability to articulate and understand them.

5. The process of reflecting upon and articulating your values and beliefs is not an exercise to be carried out once; it is

an ongoing process to visit and revisit throughout your work with this manual and your work as an educator.

Exercise 1: Exploring your values and beliefs

a) Circle five traits and characteristics that you would like children to be or to have as a result of their experience with you.

adventurous	appreciation of beauty	determined
affectionate	inquisitive	energetic
polite	respectful	friendly
altruistic	self-starter	obedient
caring	sense of humour	spontaneous
honest	industrious	persistent
assertive	creative	proud
confident	independent thinker	risk taker
cheerful	desire to excel	open-minded

Bloom, P. (2003) *Leadership in Action: How effective directors get things done.* Lake Forest, IL: New Horizons (p. 102). (Reprinted from *Blueprint for action: Achieving center-based change through staff development*, pp. 232-33, by Bloom, P.J., Sheerer, M., & Britz, J., 1991, Lake Forrest, IL: New Horizons (Assessment Tool #18).

b) Write each of your five choices on one of the lines below. Consider what each one really means to you by defining it and explaining it in the space below the line on which it is written.

i) _____

ii) _____

iii) _____

iv) _____

v) _____

c) Transfer the five traits/characteristics that you identified in Exercise 1 a) to the first column of the table below. Consider how and where these traits currently exist in different parts of your program. The table can be used as a guide for this exercise or you may wish to develop your own table on a separate sheet of paper.

Trait/ Characteristic	Physical Environment of Classroom	Teacher/Child Interactions	Free Play	Teacher-planned Experiences	Other Parts of Program

d) Transfer the five traits/characteristics that you identified in Exercise 1 a) to the first column of the table below. Consider how and where you would like to strengthen your current support of them in different parts of your program. The table can be used as a guide for this exercise or you may wish to develop your own table on a separate sheet of paper.

Trait/ Characteristic	Physical Environment of Classroom	Teacher/Child Interactions	Free Play	Teacher-planned Experiences	Other Parts of Program

Exercise 2: Identifying your values and beliefs

Use the chart found on the following page, titled "Things People Value," to identify values that are important to you. Circle 10 to 15 of the values listed, and answer the following questions. (You will need a separate piece of paper to carry out this exercise.)

1. Describe what each of the values identified means to you.

2. Indicate why each of the values identified is important to you.

3. Discuss how each of the values identified is connected to your work as an educator.

4. Discuss how the values identified influence your curriculum.

Things People Value		
Accountability	Fairness	Positive attitude
Achievement	Family	Power
Adventure	Forgiveness	Prestige
Aesthetics	Freedom	Privacy
Affiliation	Friendships	Recognition
Altruism	Happiness	Reliability
Beauty	Harmony	Responsibility
Challenge	Honesty	Security
Change	Independence	Self-control
Collaboration	Innovation	Self-expression
Community	Integrity	Self-respect
Compensation	Intellectual stimulation	Service
Competence	Intimacy	Social justice
Competition	Justice	Social relationships
Cooperation	Knowledge	Spiritual growth
Creativity	Learning	Stability
Decisiveness	Logic	Teamwork
Democracy	Loyalty	Tolerance
Diversity	Mutual respect	Tradition
Efficiency	Nature	Tranquility
Environment	Neatness	Trust
Equity	Open communication	Variety
Excellence	Perseverance	Wealth
Excitement	Personal growth	Wisdom

Adapted Bloom, P. (2003). *Leadership in action: How effective directors get things done* (p. 21). Lake Forest, IL: New Horizons.

Exercise 3: Values journal

You will need a blank notebook to write in during this exercise and to refer to as you work through this manual. You will also need to read all six steps to prepare your journal. There are samples provided to help you in getting prepared.

1. Number the first 20 pages in your journal 1-20. Odd-numbered pages should have an even-numbered page facing it (i.e., page 1 and page 2 should be facing each other).

2. Refer to Exercise 2, and circle 10 values that you have. Transfer each of the 10 values as a heading on a corresponding, odd-numbered page. For example, write the first value as a heading on page 1, the second value as a heading on page 3 and so on, until you get to page 19.

3. Once you have completed writing your values on the odd-numbered pages, write out your beliefs associated with each of the values under the appropriate heading. The odd-numbered pages of your journal should resemble the sample below.

Odd-numbered journal pages

Page 1 ———————————————————————— Page number

Teamwork ——————————————— Value

Sharing planning time
Sharing information about children
Working together to change classroom environment involves cooperation and consideration of one another

Beliefs

4. Divide the even-numbered pages of your journal to resemble the following sample.

Even-numbered journal pages

Page 2	
Observation of Classroom Experience	My Feelings

5. After you have reviewed your selected values and beliefs, take note of your classroom experiences and observe the experiences of the children with whom you work for one full week. When you observe something that relates to one of the values or beliefs identified on an odd-numbered page, record that observation on the even-numbered page facing it. Next, record your feelings about the observed experience beside it and under the heading "My Feelings." Some observed classroom experiences may relate to more than one value or belief.

6. At the end of one week, review the information you have recorded in your journal. Were you able to observe and record classroom events to correspond with all of the values and beliefs identified? Were some easier to observe and record than others? If yes, why do you think that may be the case? Consider the feelings that you experienced during the recorded situations. Do you notice a trend of any kind (e.g., happy when children do what you expect, excited when children engage in something you had not considered, disappointed when children behave in a manner contrary to your directions)?

Constructivism in Early Childhood Settings

In a constructivist classroom, your knowledge of child development and your understanding of the children in your classroom (based upon your observations) influences your approach to curriculum development and curriculum implementation. They determine your decisions as to who initiates curriculum ideas, when during the program these ideas are introduced, in what direction they take, and how these ideas emerge.

Constructivism in early childhood settings is realized when you, as an educator, demonstrate thoughtful consideration, earnest design, and sincere commitment to the principles of constructivism. Largely influenced by your values and beliefs, your views of children -how they learn, as well as what they are capable of doing- form the basis of your commitment to the principles of constructivism. These views provide guidance for designing your physical classroom environment; developing curriculum content; implementing your program; interacting with children, colleagues, and parents; and developing relationships in your classroom.

In order for you to move forward in realizing constructivism in early childhood settings, it is important to become familiar with views about children and about curricula that are reflective of constructivist principles.

View of children

In a classroom inspired by a constructivist framework, educators view children as:

1. Competent, curious, and motivated learners.

2. Individuals who bring valuable knowledge, ideas, and experiences about their physical and social world to the classroom.

3. Individuals who begin to make sense of their world from the moment they are born.

4. Active learners (i.e., learning by doing) and social learners (i.e., learning through communication with others).

5. Individuals who come to their programs influenced by family, gender, culture, and previous experiences.

6. Individuals with a variety of learning styles and ways of understanding and constructing knowledge.

For example, based on what you observe, you may set out materials such as clay and fall gourds for children to explore and perhaps engage in some form of art activity. As the children arrive and view the clay, one of the children, William, declares, "I'm going to make a church!" He demonstrates purpose, intent, and meaning as he begins to construct his church from clay.

It quickly becomes obvious to you that William has had some experience that led him to choose this topic for his exploration of clay. As you observe him engaged with the clay, you note that he has a great deal of prior knowledge about the architecture of churches. This knowledge is reflected in the language that he uses to describe his clay construction (e.g., spires, stained glass windows). You also note that other children have joined the activity and are contributing their knowledge and interpretations of churches to the situation.

By encouraging children to investigate topics in ways that make sense to them, you nurture their natural curiosity and tendency to construct knowledge and understanding through meaningful ways. Children learn from each other and increase their understanding of concepts when their ideas are respected and their pursuit of theories is supported. Collectively, these views make your classroom an enriching and stimulating place to learn and build relationships based on respect and trust.

Exercise 4: Connecting your values

a) In order to carry out this exercise you will need to refer to any one of the previous exercises that you have completed (Exercise 1, 2, or 3).

i) Consider the views of children listed in the following chart that are characteristic of a constructivist framework.

ii) Review the values you identified in Exercise 1, 2, or 3, as being important to you.

iii) Match the values you identified to the view(s) of children listed.

iv) Consider the ones that match and reflect on how and why they match.

v) Consider the views of children that you did not find a match to in your identified values. Why do you think that may be the case?

Exercise 4a) continued.

Views of Children Characteristic of a Constructivist Framework	Your Identified Values
Motivated learners who are competent and curious.	
Individuals who bring valuable knowledge, ideas, and experiences about their physical and social world to the classroom.	
Individuals who are beginning to make sense of their world from the moment they are born.	
Individuals capable of active learning and social learning.	
Individuals who come to their programs influenced by family, gender, culture, and previous experiences.	
Individuals with a variety of learning styles and ways of constructing understanding.	

b) Consider the views of children listed and record concrete examples of how you support those views in your classroom. Be specific.

Views of Children Characteristic of a Constructivist Framework	Concrete Classroom Examples
Motivated learners who are competent and curious.	
Individuals who bring valuable knowledge, ideas, and experiences about their physical and social world to the classroom.	
Individuals who are beginning to make sense of their world from the moment they are born.	
Individuals capable of active learning and social learning.	
Individuals who come to their programs influenced by family, gender, culture, and previous experiences.	
Individuals with a variety of learning styles and ways of constructing understanding.	

In a classroom inspired by a constructivist framework, educators view curriculum in the following manner:

- All aspects of the program are considered essential parts of the curriculum.

In an early childhood setting, children are involved in a variety of experiences during the course of their day. Some of these include free play, small group time, circle time, snack, lunch, rest, bathroom routine, outdoor time, and occasional field trips. For children, learning occurs throughout the whole day. All parts of the program present equal opportunities for children to demonstrate what they value, find interesting, and want to know more about. It is important that you view and use all parts of your program as potential learning opportunities that can help stimulate children's interests and extend their knowledge.

- Curriculum is designed to empower children to extend their knowledge and to construct meaningful understanding of their social and physical world.

Curriculum ideas are based on your observations of children and are designed to facilitate their discovery of new information by actively engaging them in the discovery process. For example, you may observe a child attempting to problem solve how he could fasten four tires he constructed out of play dough onto an egg-carton car that he created in the art area. You may encourage him to consider what materials you have available in the classroom that make things stick together. He may suggest using glue, tape, or a stapler. You may provide these materials and facilitate his use of each one until he discovers which one works best. By supporting his attempts to actively explore the various solutions to this problem, you extend his knowledge of the properties of each of the materials in a meaningful way and empower him to find a solution.

- The classroom community (i.e., peers and adults in a specific setting who learn together) is the source of curriculum.

Curriculum ideas spring from common interests and shared experiences of your classroom community rather than from predetermined themes. For example, you may observe children showing an interest in a bulldozer that was moving cement blocks on the playground and as a result may add small and large toy bulldozers to the block corner. This addition to the blocks of various sizes that are already in the block corner, may allow children who are playing there to discover the physical energy required by a small bulldozer to move blocks of different sizes, and compare that with the physical energy required by a large bulldozer. By creating learning opportunities that emphasize and extend children's experiences and interests you increase their potential to develop meaningful knowledge and understanding.

- Curriculum emerges from the children and from what they value, find interesting, and want to know more about.

As children participate in program routines, interact with peers, and use materials, they communicate their existing interests and competencies. These existing interests and competencies provide you, as an educator, with valuable information as to what direction the curriculum may take. For example, a child may come into the classroom wearing new shoes. Several of the other children may notice the new shoes and a discussion might take place between the children regarding where shoes are bought, the process of trying on new shoes, and paying for new shoes. As an educator who witnesses these interactions, you support and extend them by weaving a curriculum around them. As a result, the children may set-up a shoe store in the classroom, visit a shoe store, compare the size of everyone's shoes and design a chart to record this information, or invite a shoe-maker to the classroom to learn how shoes are made. As the curriculum emerges and evolves, it diverges along new paths as children make choices and connections, encounter new problems, formulate solutions, and enrich their learning experience.

- In this emergent curriculum, both adults and children take initiative and make decisions.

As noted above, the curriculum that you develop and implement should be based upon the interests and family background of the children in your classroom and your knowledge of child development. In addition, you may want to develop a partnership with the parents so as to draw upon their expertise and knowledge in the community. This collaborative approach to curriculum development and implementation creates a culture that reflects the values and interests of the classroom community. For instance, in the previous example where children's interest in new shoes emerges into curriculum ideas, you, as an educator may purposefully guide the curriculum by making suggestions based on what you know to be necessary for children's learning and development. As children show an interest in each other's shoes, you may express curiosity about whose shoes are the longest. This may lead to children measuring the lengths of their shoes, placing their shoes in order from longest to shortest, and documenting their results on a chart. When parents come to pick up their children, the chart may elicit conversation from parents and lead you to learn that one of the parents works in a shoe maker shop. You may invite this parent to bring some tools to the classroom and demonstrate how shoes are made. While you and the parents can, and should, provide and extend curriculum ideas, the direction these ideas take continues to be largely determined by the interests of the children. So, if no interest is shown in the shoe maker demonstration by the children, it would not require further extension into the program.

- Not all children have to be involved in the same curriculum activities at the same time.

As individuals, children have many different interests and may not investigate the same topic in the same way. In the example of the shoe interest, there may be a significant number of children whose focus is on exploring shoes, but the way in which they carry out their exploration may be different. Some may create a shoe store, others may measure shoe lengths, whereas others may be more interested in a completely different topic. The flow of the curriculum should be sufficiently flexible to allow children the opportunity to develop their interests and to work together in small or large groups, or to work individually.

- Play and hands-on learning experiences are essential to the development of children's understanding and their constructing of knowledge.

Children are naturally drawn to play and to experiences that involve the use of concrete materials. As they manipulate play materials they act on their intentions, test hypothesis, and construct new knowledge in meaningful ways that are relevant to their unique situations. As an educator, you support children in this process by participating in their play, presenting additional materials, asking thought-provoking questions that encourage them to consider different perspectives, and providing verbal suggestions for using materials in new and different ways. For example, you may observe children engaged in pretend cooking activities in the house area. You may enter their play by knocking and asking if you could join them for lunch. Once in the play situation, you may inquire how they made the soup they are serving and ask if you could have the recipe. You may also tell them that you brought some chocolate chips and are wondering if they could use them in their cooking.

- The curriculum provides a vehicle for relationship building between children and their peers as well as children and their educators.

The curriculum in a constructivist model is negotiated among all members of the classroom community and is shaped by their contributions. It provides opportunities for the development of positive and trusting relationships, and respect for members. All ideas in a constructivist setting are valued and explored requiring the classroom community to work together, to negotiate, and to compromise. Perspective-taking is built into the curriculum, which allows children to experience learning, to respect each other's interests, and to value their competencies.

For example, often children have very strong ideas about how things should be done or what topics should be investigated. In one classroom there may be several children interested in the same topic with several ideas as to how it could be explored. In addition, you, as an educator, may also have your own ideas about how you would like to proceed with the investigation. In a constructivist classroom, this is viewed as positive, as it presents a concrete opportunity for perspective-taking. You and the children may each take turns describing what you would like to do. Working together you decide upon a course of action that may result in several variations that all explore the same topic. Children learn that there are many ways to engage in learning about a topic. For example, the child who was interested in looking at the bulldozer and talking about it, is surprised to learn that there are books and videos about bulldozers and sits with rapt attention as you read a large picture book about construction equipment (e.g., Richard Scarry, *Cars and Trucks and Things That Go,* 1976, 2005).

- Curriculum decisions are reflected upon by educators and those reflections provide a springboard for new curriculum decisions.

Through the process of observation, interpretation, and reflection, you can develop an in-depth understanding of who the children are as individuals, what roles they assume in the group, and how best to ensure that both their individuality and their strengths as members of a classroom are nurtured and developed to their full potential. This understanding is the cornerstone of developing new curriculum ideas, extending familiar ones, and negotiating the direction of the curriculum.

- Knowledge about children's development is one of the features that guides curriculum decisions.

Your knowledge of child development helps you frame interpretations of children's behaviour that you have observed and assists you in making classroom decisions. Developmental milestones and typical patterns of behaviour can be used as a guide for understanding normal patterns of development. For all aspects of development there are ranges within which the milestones reached are considered to be normal. For example, the average age when children begin crawling is 7 months, whereas the range for the development of this skill is from 5-11 months. So, if a child is not yet crawling at 12 months you should be observing the child closely for evidence of pre-crawling behaviours. By so doing you may question whether the child should be referred to a pediatrician or whether the development of this skill could be promoted through certain daily exercises. The principles of child development knowledge that play a central role in a constructivist classroom are:

1. Children's learning and development are integrated. The child develops as a whole and emphasis is not upon the growth of a particular skill set or subject.

2. All areas of development are interconnected and all have equal importance in a child's life.

3. Displays of greater competency in a particular area by a child may be used as a means of nurturing opportunities for development in other areas.

4. Development is the result of a child's experience and maturation. Over the course of development, children's thought processes and abilities become increasingly complex. This increased complexity in thought combined with children's life experiences and their interactions with people, objects and interesting materials leads to further development.

5. Children's development is supported when opportunities to build on existing competencies are provided. The adult provides opportunities for children to engage in activities that are stimulating and challenging, yet not so difficult that children become frustrated or disinterested.

6. Even though children's development may be characterized by stages, each individual will develop at his or her own rate.

7. Global development is supported and is not broken down into discrete skills or taught as specific skills. You must see the child as a whole and focus on ways of integrating the acquisition of certain sets of skills (e.g., printing the alphabet, counting) into meaningful and relevant activities and projects.

8. Children's early experiences have a significant impact on the rest of their development as they build on their successes and use them as a springboard for subsequent learning opportunities.

- Relationships are at the forefront of curriculum implementation.

Positive relationships are cultivated in an atmosphere of respect and trust where all members of the learning community have a voice. As members of the classroom community, children are given choices and encouraged to engage in collaboration with peers and educators. In such an environment you, as an educator, demonstrate genuine interest in children, their intentions, and their individual approaches to learning and thinking. You use children's prior experiences and current classroom experiences to get to know what they like and dislike, how they respond to activities, and how they prefer to learn. This allows you to determine the appropriate ways to scaffold their thinking and understand their thought processes. Rather than providing the "right answer," you allow children to develop their own theories, develop their own answers to questions, and communicate these ideas to you and to their peers.

Daily classroom practices

There are several elements of curriculum that are directly related to your day-to-day classroom practices that require discussion as separate sections. These are: communication, physical classroom environment, classroom schedules, activities as learning opportunities, and behaviour guidance.

Communication

In a constructivist setting, communication is an important vehicle that conveys your respect and acceptance of children and their ideas and also expands learning opportunities. When speaking with children, you are aware of both spoken and body language and express yourself in a calm, positive tone. As well, you recognize your role as a model for children's language development and utilize grammatically correct language.

- Natural conversations are the language of the classroom.

Natural conversations involve speaking to children in ways that are respectful and appropriate to the situation and using language that is accurate and reflective of the concepts being explored. In a natural conversation, the adult and child take turns asking questions or making comments and listen respectfully to the responses. The questions posed (by an educator) could be to clarify, to increase comprehension, or to facilitate more complex thinking and problem solving. The child's answers should be digested and reflected upon to enable further engagement in the process of constructing new knowledge and understanding. For example, the child hears a fire truck going down the street with its siren wailing and states that it makes a lot of noise. The teacher replies that it does make a lot of noise and then comments that when people hear a noise like that they usually stop and look to see where the noise is coming from.

- Educators engage in active listening while interacting with children.

Active listening allows you to understand children better and to engage in the roles of both learner and educator. Active listening involves paraphrasing, sharing understanding, accepting ideas, and exchanging theories. By paraphrasing the child's statement you ensure that you have understood what he/she is saying. The goal is to establish a shared understanding with the child about what is happening or what the child is thinking about. Active listening involves open-mindedness and a willingness to suspend judgment as you listen and accept that all ideas and questions expressed by children are relevant to their exploration of various concepts. Active listening is a way to exchange theories and hypothesize together about why things happen. By listening to the language that children use and by watching their body language you have a better idea of how they understand the situation. In the process, you demonstrate that their ideas are valued and their experiences are worthy of dialogue and exploration.

Let's repeat the example of the child who hears a fire truck going down the street with its siren wailing and states that it makes a lot of noise. The teacher paraphrases the child's statement by saying "You think it makes a lot of noise?" This gives the child, Emily, the opportunity to confirm that the educator has understood her statement correctly by answering yes or no. By listening to the tone of the child's voice and watching her body language, the educator may recognize that the child is showing evidence of being afraid. The educator can then ask the girl how the sound is making her feel? When the child responses that the siren makes her afraid, the educator can paraphrase this response and then ask for reasons why it makes her afraid. She then answers that last night there was a fire alarm in her apartment building and the fire trucks came and made a lot of scary noise. She was asleep when this happened and it made her feel afraid. The educator can then go on to talk about the child's feelings and help her cope with this frightening experience.

- Questioning

In a constructivist classroom, questions are aimed at helping children articulate ideas clearly and are designed to help them arrive at their own solutions. Questions are not posed merely for the sake of asking a question. Open-ended questions that do not have a single right or wrong answer and that elicit description, detail, and thinking play an important role in furthering children's knowledge and their critical and analytical thinking skills. Since open-ended questions do not demand a right or wrong answer, these types of questions remove the stress of having to be correct, and provide a safer situation in which the children can be creative and wonder about possibilities. Examples of open-ended questions are: "Why do you think that happened?" or "What else could you have done?"

Close-ended questions that have a right or wrong answer also have a role in a constructivist classroom; however, they are used sparingly with a specific purpose in mind. For instance, you may wish to verify whether a child has learned the label/name for a particular animal and may use the opportunity that arises during story time to ask what animal, in the picture book that you are reading, is standing in the river drinking water.

Exercise 5: Child development and the curriculum

a) On the following chart, consider the principles of child development that have been identified as playing a central role in a constructivist curriculum. On the next page provide evidence of how each is realized in your classroom.

Principles of Child Development	Evidence in Current Curriculum
All areas of development are interconnected.	
All areas have equal importance in a child's growth and development.	
A child's competency in a particular area is used to support development in other areas.	
Children's real-life experiences and interactions with people, objects and interesting materials support further development.	
Children's competencies are recognized and opportunities are created for children to engage in stimulating and challenging activities that are not so difficult that children become frustrated or disinterested.	
Although children's development may be characterized by stages, individuals are helped to develop at their own rate.	
The child is seen as a whole and there is focus on the integration of certain sets of skills (e.g., printing the alphabet, counting) into meaningful and relevant activities and projects.	

b) On the following chart, indicate a plan of how you would support those principles that are not currently present in your classroom, and further strengthen those that are present

Principles of Child Development	Changes/additions to the Curriculum to Address these Principles
All areas of development are interconnected.	
All areas have equal importance in a child's growth and development.	
A child's competency in a particular area is used to support development in other areas.	
Children's real-life experiences and interactions with people, objects and interesting materials support further development.	
Children's competencies are recognized and opportunities are created for children to engage in stimulating and challenging activities that are not so difficult that children become frustrated or disinterested.	
Although children's development may be characterized by stages, individuals are helped to develop at their own rate.	
The child is seen as a whole and there is focus on the integration of certain sets of skills (e.g., printing the alphabet, counting) into meaningful and relevant activities and projects.	

Physical classroom environment

A well-designed, culturally rich, and stimulating environment takes on the role of co-educator in a constructivist curriculum model. It is designed with children in mind and supports their play intentions, offers opportunities for inquiry-based learning and concept development, and allows curriculum ideas to naturally emerge from children's interactions. Inquiry-based learning involves finding answers to questions derived from experiences, interests, or curiosity. This construction of knowledge and understanding may have been stimulated by materials in the classroom.

- For this type of learning to occur the environment should offer many interesting, open-ended (i.e., materials that do not have a specific way in which they can be used such as sand, water, or play dough), and thought-provoking materials for children to express their ideas as well as generate and test theories about the world around them.

Materials that promote creative thinking and diverse ways of knowing should always be available to children throughout the classroom. These materials should not be included for the isolated concepts they promote, but for their potential to support overall learning. To ignite a child's sense of wonder the materials may be common objects such as toilet paper rolls, empty boxes, or pieces of differently textured cloth. They may be objects that you picked up at a garage sale, or flea market, and at the time you many not even be sure how they will be used or for what they may be used. As long as the materials are safe and interesting, children will devise various creative uses for them. To help you select open-ended and thought-provoking materials, you may consider asking yourself, "I wonder what the children might do with this material?" If you can generate several answers to your question, you may have found an interesting material to add to your classroom.

For example, you may find some interesting plastic tubing at a garage sale that you decide to purchase and bring to the classroom to place in the block corner. After the children explore the tubing, some may decide to combine it with cardboard that is already there and race small cars, experimenting with the relationship between speed and length of the hoses. They may then decide to add to the collection of materials using items such as marbles and small plastic bears. You may support their hypotheses testing by encouraging them to explore other materials in the classroom and not limiting their curiosity and ideas by requiring them to keep materials in particular centers or areas of the classroom.

- Constructivist classrooms reveal evidence of children's participation in the room arrangement, material choices, and general ownership of the classroom.

While the curriculum reflects children's areas of interest and competencies, the room design and material selection should reflect the children's interests and curiosity. Accordingly, in a constructivist classroom, the environment is one that the children can relate to and can have a say in how it should be arranged. Evidence of this may be the way materials are displayed or the presence of particular learning centers. For example, many children prefer to stand as they work at a table but prefer to sit when painting at an easel so, contrary to what adults may expect, there may be no chairs around the tables but two or more at the easel. Children may prefer to lie down on the floor to draw so you may have to provide comfortable pillows and clipboards for drawing, but no conventional writing centre. The environment should reflect the children's interests and learning styles. As a result, the arrangement may challenge traditional images of what an early childhood classroom should look like.

- Children contribute both directly and indirectly to the arrangement of classroom space.

As children's play develops, their use of classroom space may change over time. Making decisions about how the space is arranged or rearranged should be done in consultation with the children. For example, if the children in your classroom are all vying for space in the "private area," you may consult with them and guide them to arrive at a solution to satisfy all. Together you may decide that more private spaces are needed and you may empower the children by supporting them in creating more niches in the classroom where they can be alone or with another peer. Engaging in the creation of these spaces may be continued over several days and may include opportunities to decorate their spaces and to visit one another's private spaces. Space may be arranged and rearranged as children and their interests grow and develop.

In a more indirect way, you may observe children playing in a space that is too small to accommodate all of their ideas. For example, you may observe a group of ten children playing in the block corner and experiencing difficulty in the space. You may be concerned about their safety, but rather than simply limiting the number of children in the space, you may consider how you could facilitate their problem solving and support their play intentions. You may encourage them to consider solutions to their problem that may result in their rearranging the shelves to enlarge the space and accommodate everyone.

- Classrooms reflect the personalities and backgrounds of the children and educators as well as who they are in terms of language, culture, and interests.

Children come to your classroom with a wealth of experience, a culture, a language, and interests to which they are connected. For example, 3-year-old Benny may have often brought up the topic of his cat during his daily conversations with you and his classmates. Since his cat is clearly important to him, you may encourage him to bring in a photo of his cat for the classroom. You may then place the photo in a simple wood frame and display it prominently in the class.

- An uncluttered and well-organized environment is a place of investigation.

Children thrive in spaces where materials are easily located. An orderly room with materials that are visible and within easy reach encourages children to capitalize on their emerging ideas. If children have to search for materials, ideas are sometimes abandoned possibly leading to frustration. When materials are easily visible and accessible, imagination and problem solving are more likely to flourish.

- A variety of textures/sensory rich/aesthetically pleasing materials are evident.

The materials you incorporate into the classroom require a great deal of consideration as children channel their ideas through these materials. Children enjoy authentic materials that speak to their senses and have interesting properties. Many of these resources can be easily found from a variety of sources in the natural world and the community. You can easily enlist the help of parents and children to procure and organize these materials.

- Children's work is attractively and thoughtfully displayed.

By attractively displaying children's creations, you show respect for their efforts and communicate to the community at large the message that their work is valued. Children gain a sense of pride in their accomplishments and realize that their ideas are taken seriously. For example, you may consider making frames out of construction paper as a way to display children's art work, or by folding over a small piece of construction paper and making name plates for their three-dimensional art work.

- Evidence of documentation and children's thinking is embedded within the classroom.

This concept is particularly important in constructivist settings for it serves a variety of purposes. Not only does it serve to preserve memories for children and for you, it also shows an evolution of children's ideas. Documentation illustrates how ideas were conceived and how children's development of ideas has evolved over time. You and the children can revisit the documentation to extend investigations or embark on new curriculum ideas. (The documentation process is presented in section four of the manual.)

- Outdoor space and the neighboring environment is an extension of the learning environment.

Educators ought to use the natural space surrounding their classrooms as an important component of the curriculum and allow everyday experiences to extend the learning process. For example, when several preschoolers demonstrate wonder and fascination with the lines they created on paper in the art centre, you may take them outside with riding toys after it rains. The children may ride their vehicles enthusiastically through the puddles creating lines on the dry pavement. The powerful connections between the lines created in the classroom and the lines created by the riding vehicles extend and strengthen their learning.

Exercise 6: Physical classroom environment: Favourite space/Least favourite space

Consider your physical classroom environment and answer the following questions.

Favourite Classroom Space	Least Favourite Classroom Space
What is your favourite space in the classroom?	What is your least favourite space in the classroom?
Describe your favourite space in the classroom.	Describe your least favourite space in the classroom. .
How does it make you feel when you are in your favourite space in the classroom?	How does it make you feel when you are in your least favourite space in the classroom?
Why do you think you feel that way?	Why do you think you feel that way?

What could you change about your least favourite space in the classroom that would improve it?

Exercise 7: Physical classroom environment: Stimulating materials

This exercise will ask you to consider the current status of the materials in your classroom, to indicate how you would strengthen the type and organization of the materials, and to consider how you would introduce any new materials.

a) Consider the type of materials in your current classroom and how they are organized and presented to children.

Evidence of Interesting, Open-ended, Thought-provoking Materials	Evidence of Textured, Sensory-rich, Aesthetically-pleasing Materials	Evidence of How Materials are Stored in an Organized Way

b) What changes would you make to strengthen the type and organization of materials in your classroom? In considering new materials, think about materials that can be received as donations, purchased at garage sales and second hand stores, as well as purchased at teacher supply stores.

Ideas for Adding Interesting, Open-ended, Thought-provoking Materials	Ideas for Adding Textured, Sensory-rich, Aesthetically-pleasing Materials	Ideas for Making the Organizational System More Effective.

c) Now that you have identified materials that can be added to your classroom and new ways of presenting those materials to enhance children's learning, develop a plan of how you would introduce these materials into your classroom. In developing your plan, consider the following two principles of constructivist classrooms.

- Constructivist classrooms have evidence of children's participation in the room arrangement, material choices, and general ownership of the classroom.

- Children contribute both directly and indirectly to the arrangement of classroom space.

Material	Children's Contribution to the Plan and its Implementation	Your Contribution to the Plan and its Implementation

Program schedules

In a constructivist classroom the educator creates a schedule that takes into account that children's learning occurs in a variety of social settings, both indoors and outdoors. Social settings include large and small group experiences, one-on-one interactions, and time to work alone. The schedule also recognizes that children require a certain amount of stability and predictability in their daily lives, but includes times for children to carry out learning activities according to their interests. Consequently, the schedule provides a framework for how the day unfolds and balances the program and children's needs. It utilizes free-play time as a central feature.

- Daily schedules are formulated as a framework for how the day's events are organized.

As daily schedules facilitate the flow of the day, you should give careful consideration to time frames allocated to particular events and to the sequence of those events. A rushed schedule can create stress for both you and the children. Inflexible time periods that are too short and that allow only limited opportunity for responding to children's interests or their requests to revisit topics and strengthen their understanding are not recommended. There are some time periods that are connected to general centre schedules or designed to meet children's physical needs (e.g., lunch, rest time). However, the remainder of the scheduled time is within your control and should be designed to flow around the central feature of free-play time.

For example, you may introduce the concept of open snack to children. This allows children to make their own decisions about when to have snack during the free-play period. Therefore, children have a longer period of time for investigation and play and make their own decision about when to eat snack. This is helpful when children are engaged in in-depth explorations and not ready to clean up just because it is snack time.

You may also adopt a more flexible approach to planned small group activities that are available during free play. For example, you may set out a small group experience for the children, but not demand full participation in the experience by all. Those who are interested will come to the small group activity, while those who are involved in their own free play may choose to carry on with their own projects.

- Plenty of free-play time to investigate interests is provided.

The classroom schedule provides an abundance of free-play time when children are free to choose materials with which they wish to engage and to decide what they do with those materials, how much time they spend with them, and who else they will involve in their play. You may arrange the classroom so that children's projects may be left out over periods of a day or more. In this way, children may continue to work on projects over an extended period of time and build on their current knowledge and strengthen their understanding of concepts presented.

As the central feature of your schedule, free-play time may provide a springboard for spontaneous small group and circle time experiences to take place. For example, several children may be playing with play dough at the art centre. Their exploration of the play dough may result in an investigation of its properties. As a support to their play activity, you bring out the ingredients used to make the play dough and you and the children engage in a spontaneous small group experience of making more play dough in order to strengthen their understanding of how the ingredients work together to make the final product.

- Daily schedules are flexible and sensitive to the rhythms of the children.

Some children may need more time than others to complete tasks and investigate areas of interest, and some activities evolve into complex investigations that require more time than you may have originally anticipated. For example, the interest of the children in your classroom may have been captured by a small group time that you may have planned around the topic of objects that sink and float. The investigation and discussion may extend beyond the time usually allocated to small group time and may encroach on your upcoming planned circle. As a result, you take your lead from the children's interests, forfeit your planned circle for that day, and extend the small group activity. This ensures that children's involvement in an activity is not stopped abruptly and that new activities are not introduced when the children are still immersed and interested in a current project.

- Transitions are limited and occur naturally for children.

The classroom schedule is designed with only a few transitions that flow naturally out of children's play and interactions. By recognizing that children's individual interests guide their movement through the day, and by carefully observing them and listening to them, you learn about their needs and are able to adjust the schedule accordingly. For example, rather than dividing the morning into smaller sections of time for free-play, small group, bathroom, and snack that follow each other in an inflexible sequence, you may have one time period of free play. Within the free play time, you may set up a free-flowing snack and a free-flowing small group activity that the children can take part in whenever they choose.

Exercise 8: Daily schedules

Daily schedules are formulated as a framework for how the day's events are organized. In this exercise you are asked to indicate your current daily schedule and to consider any changes or modifications that you might make to it.

a) In the space provided below, write out your current daily schedule from the time your program begins until the time it ends. Indicate the name assigned to that part of the schedule (e.g., circle, free play) and the time allocated to that part of the schedule (e.g., 10:20 – 10:40).

Current Daily Schedule

Review the daily schedule you have written and consider the following questions.

i)   Does the schedule include plenty of free-play time for children to investigate their own interests? Are there classroom routines that interfere with children's free play? For example, are the sleeping cots being put out during this time? If yes, think about how this affects the children's play.

ii) Is the schedule flexible and sensitive to the rhythms of the children? For example, do children have an opportunity to eat snack when they are hungry or only at snack time, do they have an opportunity to participate in small group activities that are available during free play as their interests dictate, is there opportunity for activities to be carried out over several days as children's interests evolve?

iii) Is the number of transitions limited and do transitions occur naturally for children?

If you have answered "No" to any of the questions above, you may wish to reconsider your schedule and plan a new one. The next exercise may be helpful in your planning.

b) In planning your new daily schedule you may wish to begin by writing out those parts of the schedule that are connected to the functioning of the entire centre and that you may not have complete control over such as lunch, rest time, and outdoor play time.

Next consider parts of the schedule that may traditionally be carried out within a fixed time frame that requires the participation of all children, (e.g., snack, small group), but that could be redesigned to include more flexibility. For example, you may introduce a free-floating snack in the morning and the afternoon, as part of free play, that children can go to when they choose. In order to do this you may need to speak with the Director or negotiate with the cook. You may also consider introducing a small group experience within free play that children can participate in as their interests dictate.

Next consider the amount of time allocated for free play to ensure that there is plenty of opportunity for children to investigate their interests and also participate in snack and small group activities.

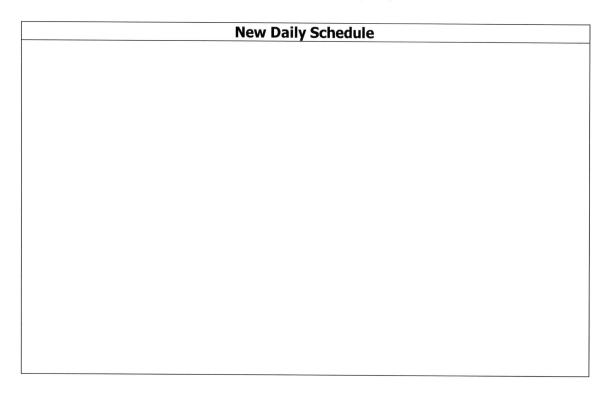

Educator-planned experiences as learning opportunities

Even though child-initiated free play is a central feature of a constructivist classroom, there is abundant opportunity for educator-planned experiences to occur. In a constructivist classroom, educator-planned experiences may take a variety of forms that require creative thinking. Some of these experiences may be planned in advance and others may emerge as a result of a teachable moment you observed during children's spontaneous play. All forms of educator-planned experiences are designed to build on children's interests and emerging capabilities, therefore it is not appropriate to plan experiences weeks and months ahead because you should be assessing children's needs and interests as they emerge.

- Group experience planned by the educator prior to implementation.

Based on your observations of children you may plan a group experience in order to extend emerging interests or concepts or introduce new concepts. Even though you may plan the framework for this experience prior to implementation, the manner in which the activity is carried out and the direction it may take will be determined by the children's interests and reactions during the group experience. In order to carry out this experience, it is essential to have a set of available materials that support your initial plan. As well, there should be a variety of additional materials in the classroom that may supplement your initial plan, which should be accessible to children. The focus of your plan and implementation should be children's learning and not a specific product.

For example, you may observe that children in your classroom are interested in making prints with their hands. You may plan a creative art experience where they print with their hands to support the concept that print-making involves dipping a form in wet paint and applying it to paper. In order to support this you provide paper and containers of thick finger paint. As the experience begins, you observe one of the children making a line of hand prints across her paper and three other children working on one paper as they sort their hand prints according to size. While this is going on, one of the children announces that he would like to use his feet. After discussing the need to place the paper and paint on the floor, he takes off his socks, dips his feet in the container, and walks across the paper. Several of the other children announce that they too would like to do this. You may get additional paper so as to support their desires and provide a big bucket of water for foot washing. You can use this extension of a planned activity as an opportunity to ask open-ended questions that will encourage the children to compare and contrast the differences between hand and foot prints.

Through their participation, active learning, and decision-making, children determine the direction their print-making experiences take and the creations that result from these experiences. When you design and implement experiences that are meaningful to children, they are motivated to participate in the process and connect with the concepts introduced.

- Enhancing the environment as an educator-planned experience.

Educator-planned experiences may also involve adding materials to the environment in order to provide additional learning opportunities. For example, you may have observed that several children in your classroom are interested in measuring objects. Rather than teaching children about measurement through a teacher planned activity, you may plan to strategically add materials into the classroom environment so that children can explore on their own initiative during free play. Some of these materials may include measuring tapes introduced into the block area, large and small weigh scales put into the house area, and rulers placed in the art area.

- Perspective taking

It is important to view learning situations from a child's perspective. To do this, you observe what children are interested in, how they like to explore their interests, what challenges they face in the pursuit of new knowledge, and how they interact with their peers. By shifting your perspective and respecting those of the learners, you appreciate that the children's interests may not reflect your own and develop creative ways of blending curriculum content with children's interests. As a result, the curriculum that emerges will be one that is based upon shared ideas, needs, and goals.

- Extending the teachable moment as a learning opportunity.

Recognizing and extending a teachable moment allows you to connect children's immediate interests with relevant learning opportunities. For example, during free play you may observe that several children playing in the art area have built three-dimensional structures and are discussing whose is the biggest. You may recognize this as a teachable moment to support mathematics-related learning opportunities. As a result, you take advantage of this moment and encourage children to tell you how they can figure out which structure is the biggest. You listen to their ideas, and identify that there appear to be different ways to measure size. As a group, you may explore measuring height with a ruler, weighing with a scale, and measuring width with a measuring tape.

Exercise 9: Educator-planned experiences as learning opportunities

a) Consider your current approach to planning and implementing learning experiences for children. In order to carry out this exercise, review the small group or circle time experiences that you planned and implemented during the last five days. In reviewing those experiences, consider the following questions:

Planning the experience

- Where did the ideas to plan the experiences come from? For example, did they come from observations of children's interests, from observations of their emerging competencies, from predetermined curriculum themes, from approaching holidays, from craft resources, etc.?
- What goals did you have in presenting these experiences? For example, did you wish to teach specific skills such as cutting with scissors, to introduce children to new classroom materials, or to focus on global aspects of development such as negotiation or literacy?
- Did you have a particular end product in mind that would be produced by children as a result of the experience? For example, was everyone to make a Thanksgiving turkey out of precut shapes?
- Did you include a variety of materials that would stimulate children's sensory exploration and inquiry skills?

Implementing the experience

- Did the children have an opportunity to use materials in a variety of ways? For example, in using glue, some children focused on exploring the properties of the material by squishing it between their fingers, and some children used the glue to make creations.
- Did the children have an opportunity to introduce additional materials or ideas to the group experience? For example,

some children brought tape from the art area to use or made suggestions of what books could be read next.

- If children made creations, were they all relatively similar (e.g., the children made a Valentine's card using pre-cut hearts), or were they unique (i.e., a wide variety of materials were available for those children who chose to make a card).

- Did you converse with all of the children as they participated in the experience?

- Did you use thought-provoking, open-ended expressions such as "How did you get your building to be so tall?" or "I wonder what would happen if..." that focused on the process of what they were doing?

- Did the children have the opportunity to share ideas with each other in a natural way during the course of the experience?

- Did the children have the opportunity to extend the experience into another part of the day, or over several days if they chose?

Following the experience

- Did you use ideas expressed by the children during one experience to connect to the next planned experience?

- Did you make additions to classroom materials as a result of any of the experiences?

b) Consider your answers to the questions in Exercise 9a) and relate them to the information found in this chapter. You may find it helpful to use the chart on the following page to organize your answers.

i)   How do your answers relate to the information presented?

ii) What have you learned about your current approach to planning and implementing learning experiences for children? How do your ideas fit with those expressed in a constructivist framework?

iii) Do you see any relationships between the answers you have provided to the questions and your values and beliefs about how children learn?

iv) If yes, identify those relationships?

v)   Identify any changes you would consider making in your current approach to planning and implementing learning experiences?

My Answers to the Questions Regarding Planned Learning Experiences.	How My Answers Relate to Information found in "Constructivism in early childhood settings."	How My Answers Relate to My Previously Identified Values and Beliefs.	Changes I Would Consider Making in my Current Approach to Planning and Implementing Learning Experiences.
Planning the experience			
Implementing the experience			
After the experience			

Behaviour guidance

The focus in a constructivist classroom is on the process of guiding children to develop self-discipline, self-respect, and empathy towards others. You provide children with opportunities to develop these skills through modeling and by implementing strategies that facilitate children's success. This may come in the form of supporting children's development of specific strategies, such as expressing their feelings in an appropriate manner, either physically or verbally. Additionally, the curriculum can be seen as a collaborator in promoting children's success at social problem solving by using planning strategies to create a positive learning environment (e.g., when introducing a new dollhouse include enough props so that the children can engage in group pretend play). You focus on building positive relationships with children so that they trust you and feel comfortable, which will encourage them to explore the environment. In a constructivist environment, you view challenging behaviors as opportunities for children to learn about and understand their positive and negative emotions. You guide children to develop positive ways of coping with their emotions, especially during interactions with their playmates.

- Creation of a positive learning environment that minimizes challenging behaviours and children's frustration.

In recognizing that group interactions may be challenging at times for some children, you design a learning environment that promotes success and maximizes their potential to solve social problems. For example, you create a physical environment that is stimulating and reflective of children's play interests. Such an environment is clearly organized and includes adequate space within play centres for children to move about and build structures without unnecessarily interrupting each other. You plan learning experiences and activities that are open-ended so that they can be carried out in various ways, are based on your observations of the children's play, and build on their interests and emerging capabilities. You include a classroom schedule that is flexible, with few transitions, and this allows curriculum ideas to emerge from children's spontaneous play experiences. By paying attention to these factors, you will create a rich, hands-on environment that will encourage children to be fully engaged with the materials and their peers, thus minimizing opportunities for conflict.

- Conflict can provide an opportunity for children to develop social problem solving and negotiation skills.

Conflicts are a part of all social relationships and the key is guiding children to recognize this and to solve their social problems in positive ways. Thus, it is important to provide children with real and concrete opportunities for solving social problems by using critical thinking skills. Your goal is to engage the children in problem solving so that they come up with a reasonable solution rather than you always providing the end solution. For example, when approaching the block area you hear two children arguing over a toy truck and see them pulling at the same truck. At this point, you act as a guide to facilitate the children's solution to the problem rather than solving it for them. This can be accomplished by asking the children what the problem is and how they might solve the problem themselves. You also help them to see each other's point of view and to express their emotions in positive ways (e.g., "Rather than yelling, let's talk about this in a calm way. How should we begin? What about starting with talking about why you are upset?").

- Educators examine children's behaviours as a means of understanding intent.

You explore the context of the situation in which challenging behaviours occur by talking about it with the children. In this way you avoid making assumptions about what has happened and why it has happened. By seeking information and thinking clearly about why a child initiated or engaged in a particular behaviour you try to understand his/her desire or motivation. As well, you try to help the children understand each other's point of view. For example, you may observe one child kicking another and grabbing a toy truck from him. By speaking with the children you may discover that the child who did the kicking was playing with the truck first, that he put it down and turned around to look for the male figurine that belonged in the truck, and in that time, the other child had picked up the truck. Once this information is shared you may be able to help the two children engage in a discussion about ownership and fairness, and subsequently about sharing and cooperation. By helping to expose the reason why the child had picked up the truck, (i.e., he believed that the first child was finished playing with it), you have material to work with. You can guide the child who picked up the truck to ask his classmate if he was finished and help the child who did the kicking to find a more appropriate way of expressing his desire to continue playing with the truck. It also may be an appropriate opportunity to facilitate a turn-taking approach to using the truck so that both children have the chance to play with it. Or you may encourage the second child to find another truck and to join his classmate in constructing a garage for the two trucks. In this way, you encourage the children to solve the problem in positive ways and also promote joint play.

- Educators believe that children are competent and have the skills to work out issues with peers and adults.

You recognize that children have many skills and competencies that they bring to every learning situation. You provide support and guidance as they make sense of these skills and apply them in social problem solving situations, as we have outlined above. By acting as a facilitator, you can engage them in reconciliation and help them to use their reasoning skills so as to initiate solutions that are positive (i.e., where both children are satisfied with the outcome).

- Children construct their own social knowledge about the world.

Children are in the process of constructing social knowledge (e.g., understanding social interactions such as how to enter a play group, different kinds of relationships such as with educators, parents, peers). Social knowledge, like the construction of other types of knowledge (e.g., mathematical, cognitive) requires some trial and error. Children frequently make mistakes as they try to understand their social world, but this is important for the process of learning. It is important to be understanding and supportive as the children struggle to make sense of social problems, particularly during conflicts with their peers.

- Educators recognize that conflict situations may heighten emotions that may challenge children's abilities to generate solutions to social problems.

In early childhood classrooms, conflict situations are often a result of a disagreement with a peer about objects, space, or rights. During conflicts, emotions are often heightened as children struggle to make their point of view known. They know what they want, but sometimes it is difficult for young children to express themselves in appropriate ways, thus they resort to behaviors that adults see as inappropriate. For example when two children are tugging at the same toy, they are both emotionally invested in wanting to use it at the same time and may resort to pushing and hitting as they attempt to claim the toy. As a result, you may indicate that you will hold the toy in your lap and will stay with them while they find a solution to the problem. As facilitator and guide in this situation, it is important to acknowledge their emotional connection to the toy (e.g., "I understand that you both like to play with this toy."). You should be supportive as they struggle to gain control of their emotions and consider alternative solutions. For example, you may say that you see that they both look upset, and that you understand that both of them see this as a favourite toy. However, hurting each other is not an appropriate way to solve the problem. So you may say "Let's find a way to solve the problem by talking and not hitting each other." Supportive statements such as these will indicate to the children that you understand how important this toy is to them. You may follow these statements with questions such as "What do you think we could do since both of you want to use this toy? Can you think of a solution that will make both of you happy?" As part of the discussion, remember to help them consider the consequences of their suggestions and that some may be more reasonable than others. For example, if one of the children gives a suggestion such as "Tell him to go home and stay there!" you may say, "I hear what you are saying and understand why you are saying that, but that is not a solution because this is his day care as well. Now, do you have another idea?"

- Educators cooperate with parents on guidance issues.

In constructivist classrooms, communication with parents occurs on a daily basis and not only when problems arise. This communication is based on respect and the mutual goal of creating positive learning experiences for all the children. You share observations with parents and engage their support in facilitating guidance issues so that all parties can work together cooperatively. For example, you observe that during the open snack Toni often walks around the room eating his snack. You encourage him to sit down while he eats, because it is a safety issue and you also want to encourage conversation with his peers who are sitting at the table. However, Toni responds that he never does that at home. In order to address this situation, you may discuss the issue with Toni's parents. In speaking with them, you may ask them about Toni's eating habits at home. You may discover that at home it is common practice for Toni to take food from the table and eat it while walking around the house or playing with his toys. You may indicate that although you understand that this is how he handles food at home, for safety reasons you are not able to support this practice in the classroom. You may discuss your specific safety concerns to further his parents' understanding of your classroom requirements, as well as to explain the social value of talking with peers at the snack table. You may then ask the parents to talk with Toni about why there may be different expectations at home and day care about where to eat food. In this way, you attempt to get the parents' cooperation and to build a partnership with them.

Exercise 10: Behaviour guidance

a) Consider the list of points regarding behaviour guidance from the section of the manual titled "Constructivism in early childhood settings." Reflect on each of the points and record your views (i.e., agreement or disagreement and why), as well as opportunities and/or challenges that you perceive in realizing each point in your current classroom environment.

Points Regarding Behavior Guidance	My Views	Opportunities that Help You Make Changes	Challenges to Change
Children construct their own social knowledge about the world (e.g., how to enter play groups, negotiating about sharing toys).			
During conflict situations, children's emotions are heightened and may get in the way of their ability to generate solutions.			
Educators work in co-operation with parents on guidance issues.			

b) Consider the challenges you have identified above in relation to behaviour guidance in your classroom. Now, reflect upon additional information that has been covered in the section "Constructivism in early childhood settings," such as curriculum, physical environment, schedules, and learning opportunities. Consider if any of that information is helpful in addressing some of these challenges.

Classroom Challenges in Realizing Constructivism in the Classroom in Relation to Behaviour Guidance	Possible Solutions through Curriculum Changes	Possible Solutions through Physical Environment Changes	Possible Solutions through Scheduling Changes	Possible Solutions through Approaches to Learning Experience Changes

Observation

Observation provides the foundation for developing a constructivist curriculum. Through observation, you should be able to determine children's interests, competencies, approaches to challenging learning situations, and reactions to success or failure. The way you interpret this information will help you plan learning experiences that will build upon what children already know and challenge them in appropriate ways to further their learning. You can use observation to determine what works best for children in a variety of situations and as evidence when discussing children's learning with other individuals. This chapter, like the others, includes exercises that will help you develop your observational skills.

For Notes

In learning how to utilize observational techniques to develop and implement a constructivist curriculum framework, it helps to consider the observation process from the following five perspectives: (a) role of observation in a constructivist classroom, (b) influences on observation, (c) preparing for observation, (d) knowledge and skills of observational techniques, and (e) knowledge and skills of interpreting observations.

The role of observation in a constructivist model

As you go through the process of developing curriculum strategies specific to your classroom situation, observations will:

1. Provide a means for determining the children's perspective on the world.

2. Provide an effective method for gathering information about each child's growth and development.

3. Enable you to gather valuable information about how the children construct knowledge and further their understanding.

4. Provide you with information to reflect upon and use in creating supportive learning environments that build upon the children's interests and what they already know. This acts as the springboard for determining the next step in furthering the child's learning and understanding of the physical and social world.

5. Assist you in determining how best to encourage the children to explore new ideas, take risks, and be problem solvers.

6. Support or endorse collaborative, working relationships by providing material for discussions.

7. Prompt you to reflect upon your own learning styles, teaching styles, and approaches to working with others (e.g., children, colleagues, families).

8. Provide information to build positive relationships with others in the learning community (i.e., educators, children, parents).

Influences on observations

The manner in which you perceive issues (e.g., children's learning, social behaviour, parental concerns) is influenced by your personal lens that has been formed and shaped by your past experiences, cultural background, values and beliefs, gender, and education. While it may not be possible to completely eliminate these influences, it is essential to be aware of them and operate in a manner that limits their effects on your perceptions as much as possible. For instance, your gender bias may influence your impression of three boys who frequently engage in loud, superhero play by moving swiftly around the room bumping into furniture and peers; you may label their behaviour as aggressive. However, when you engage in observations that are objective and carefully designed you see that the three boys are just making superhero noises and purposely missing each other as they pretend to make karate chops and elbow one another. Through this focused observation you are able to determine that the boys are engaging in rough-and-tumble (R&T) play rather than being aggressive.

Preparing for observation

Before you begin the process of observing children's behaviours, consider the following:

- What is the purpose of your observation?

Knowing what you want to observe and why will help you determine the type of technique to use, the best time to observe, and the best location from which to observe. For example, you may wish to gather information about how the children are using the dramatic play area. As you do not have a specific behavioural focus in mind, you may decide to use a running record technique that will give you a wide variety of information for you to draw upon. (Observational techniques will be discussed later in this chapter.)

- Non-participant or participant observer – your decision.

Non-participant observer
As a non-participant observer you remove yourself from the classroom action positioning yourself in a comfortable place at an appropriate distance from the target(s) of your observation. Your goal is to blend into the background of the classroom, but still be able to see facial expressions and hear verbal exchanges. As a non-participant observer you should not influence what is happening in the classroom. This may be difficult in the beginning as the children may not be accustomed to seeing you remove yourself from the on-going activity. If they approach you and initiate contact with you, it is best to inform them that you are working right now and will join them as soon as you have finished your work. When they ask you what you are doing (and they will) let them know that you are watching what is happening in the classroom and writing things down so that you do not forget. You might have to repeat this

several times before they lose interest in you and return to their play.

To facilitate becoming a non-participant observer you could speak to your Director to arrange for a substitute to work in your classroom while you observe. Or, if the classroom has two educators working as a team, you can take turns observing while your partner interacts with the children. In other cases, a viable alternative would be for you to have a colleague work in your classroom while you observe, and you can work in your colleague's classroom while your colleague observes.

Participant observer

A participant observer records observations while participating in classroom activities with the children. Children's behaviours and reactions to events that occur as you work with them are important and should be recorded on a regular basis. Recording these observations, however, while you are participating in classroom activities may be challenging and may require organization and preparation. When you observe a significant behaviour, jot it down immediately in shorthand. This will facilitate your recording and you can expand on it to include additional detail later in the day at a more convenient time. It is important to minimize the amount of time that passes between the time the behaviour occurs and the time you fill in the gaps so as to maximize accuracy and detail. In order to prepare yourself to record significant behaviours consider trying to:

1. Always have a pen on a string around your neck.

2. Keep sticky note pads or scraps of paper in your pocket or on top of shelves scattered throughout the room.

3. Create an observation space on a wall or behind a door, out of children's reach, on which you can attach sticky notes during the day.

As a participant observer it is important not to influence what is happening or prompt children in any way.

- Observe all of the children throughout the classroom.

While you may be tempted to focus your observations on children who exhibit problematic behaviours, observe parts of the program that create difficulty, or observe in response to upcoming assessment periods, it is essential to observe all of the children in every part of the classroom at different times of the day as they engage in a variety of activities. This will provide you with the opportunity to develop a more complete profile of their current interests, competencies, and emerging abilities. If you are equipped with this information you will be better able to create curriculum strategies that support their learning and development. In order to facilitate the observation of all the children, in every aspect of their classroom functioning, you should develop an organized record keeping system that includes a checklist of which children have been observed as well as the date of the observation and the activity in which the children were involved.

- Make time to review the observations on the same day they have been recorded and write the interpretations.

In response to the busy nature of most early childhood classrooms, the majority of your observations will most likely be recorded using a shorthand format. Therefore, it is essential to review your observations and fill in any gaps and details shortly after you have recorded the observations. You are more likely to remember details of what you saw on the same day the observation took place rather than a week or two later. Once you have finished reviewing your observations and the incidents are still fresh in your mind, you should take the time to interpret these observations and record them on the same sheet on which you have recorded your observations.

- Determine where you will store the observations for safekeeping and future reference.

Once an observation has been recorded and the information has been interpreted you should store the document in a file folder and place it in a locked cabinet to which no one but you has access. Confidentiality is a very important issue and the completed observation sheet should not be easily accessible to visitors to your classroom. You should determine the organizational system you will use to file the observations; you may want to store the information by date, topic, or child observed.

Important points to remember when conducting observations

- Be accurate in your recording.

For all of the observations it is important to be as accurate in your recording as possible. Listen carefully, watch the behavior or event unfold, and write as quickly as possible trying not to allow your eyes to leave the field of observation. If you miss something that you think was pivotal in the sequence of events, mark the point where you think it occurred.

- Use objective language that is a full description of what you are observing.

Be objective when describing what you are seeing. Do not include subjective or interpretive comments (e.g., he is sad, he is misbehaving). Also, try to use words that describe precisely what you are seeing (e.g., Tom *rolls* the car *back and forth* on the carpet *six times in succession*) rather than using summary words (e.g., Tom *plays* with the car).

- Try not to miss important parts of the sequence of events.

If you miss part of the sequence of events you will be left wondering how one action or another came about when you review your observations. You might develop some form of personal short hand to facilitate your recording since the language that is heard is as important as the actions that are seen. It is difficult to record both language and actions accurately without some form of shorthand.

- Record only what actually happens while you are observing.

Record only what actually happens; do not record what you would naturally expect to have happened as the result of what was said or done. For example, if child A hits child B and child B walks away, do not write that child B did not cry, as there are many other things that child B did not do as well. However, it is very important to know precisely what child B did after being hit because you may want to determine if his behaviour was appropriate for the situation and what kind of follow-up you should be engaging in with child B.

- Include basic information that is important to know for every observation recorded.

Always include the name of the child being observed, the date of the recording, the time of day, the activity, the number of children present, the adult-to-child ratio, and the atmosphere that exists just before you begin the recording.

- Observations must be interpreted in order for them to be useful.

While interpretations must be kept out of the observational recordings in order to have a precise image of what transpired during the observation, interpretations of what was seen and heard provide an important dimension in understanding what transpired and why it played out as it did. In order not to miss recording behaviors as they are observed, interpretations should be done only after the recording process has ended. When interpreting the child's words or actions, it is important to remember that we do not know for certain why the child has behaved in a particular manner so we must use words that reflect this uncertainty (e.g., seems, appears, might).

Beginning to observe

As mentioned under *Important points to remember when conducting observations*, it is essential that you record the context of the observation before beginning the actual recording. This includes noting information about the children, the classroom atmosphere, and rationale. Usually this information is included in the first three sections of your observation.

Section I: Information about children and classroom

As shown in the example in the box, below, always be certain to include: (a) the name of the child(ren) being observed, (b) the age group of child(ren), (c) the date of the recording, (d) the time of day, (e) the activity, (f) the number of children present, and (g) the educator-to-child ratio.

Example of Information about Children and Classroom

Date: May 22, 2003
Time of day: Morning
Number of children: 12   (Peggy, Bobby, Alexei, Sue, Greg, Wei, Olivia,
                          François, Luca, Arlene, Heather, Guy)
Age group: 3-3.5
Ratio: 1:6
Activity: Free play

Section II: Classroom atmosphere

To compose this section of the observational information you should look around the classroom and try to capture, in words, the overall picture of the classroom environment. Consider the lighting (e.g., bright because it is a sunny day and the sunlight is streaming into the classroom through the large picture windows), temperature (e.g., warm from the sunshine heating up the room), noise level (e.g., sounds of excitement fill the air as arriving children see that the guinea pigs are back from their visit to the vet), and impending activity (e.g., as the last few children enter the classroom they race over to the science area where the other eight children have surrounded the guinea pigs' cage that is located on a low table where all can have a clear view of the guinea pigs).

Example of Classroom Atmosphere

Atmosphere: It is a warm, sunny day and the natural light is streaming into the classroom. The children are chattering away about the arrival of the guinea pigs and sound very excited. The latecomers race into the room and join their peers who have formed a circle around the guinea pigs' cage. There seems to be some jostling for viewing space but the location of the cage on a low table means it is within the line of vision of most of the children. The educator takes out a bag of carrots and asks who would like to feed the guinea pigs.

Section III: Information about the Rationale

Before you begin to record an observation you should have good reason for selecting the topic that you wish to observe. We call this your rationale and suggest that you record your rationale for each observation. The rationale should serve to remind you about the reason you decided to do the particular observation. Sometimes, as educators we notice that a child takes an inordinate amount of time getting involved in an activity during free play and we are curious as to the reason for the child's behaviour. Thus, we would set out to explore the child's behaviour during the free play period noting whatever attempts the child makes to engage in an activity and the length of time that he/she stays with each activity.

Example of Rationale

Rationale: Every day Daniel enters the classroom and wanders from one activity area to another. Some days he takes the entire free play period wandering from one area to another looking at the activities but never settling in any one area. Today I will watch him to see if he tries to join ongoing activities and what happens when he makes attempts to join a group of peers who are already involved in play.

Exercise 11: Information about children and classroom

To carry out this exercise, look around the classroom and try to capture in words the overall picture of the classroom environment. Begin by collecting information about the children and classroom and move on to the general atmosphere of the environment.

Section I: Information about Children and Classroom

Include:
Age group of children,
Date of the recording,
Time of day,
Activity,
Number of children present, and
Educator/child ratio

Section II: Classroom Atmosphere

Consider the lighting, noise level, and impending activity.

Section III: Rationale

Describe what it is that you want to observe and why.

Observational techniques

There are several different observational techniques that will enable you to observe, record, and reflect upon what has been observed. When observing young children in classroom settings, there are different methodologies that are usually used. These include (a) narratives collected with running records and anecdotes, and (b) samples of specific behaviors collected with event samples.

Narratives

For narratives the information that you observe should be recorded longhand using a pencil and paper to reproduce, on paper, the behavioral events in the precise sequence in which they occurred. It is important to record everything that you see and hear. The type of narrative recording you decide to use, *running record* or *anecdote*, depends upon why you are observing and the type of record you want to have for future reference.

Running record

The running record is a recording of what transpires in a sequence of events; you can use words that describe the action taking place and include some adjectives and adverbs that will help you picture what was observed long after the observation has occurred. For this type of recording try to act much like a video camera focusing on the activity as it evolves. The descriptions provided should enable any reader to reconstruct the situation and the activity in full detail. For this type of recording you should remove yourself from participating with the children.

Running Record Example

Date: May 22, 2006
Time of day: Morning
Number of children: 12   (Peggy, Bobby, Alexei, Sue, Greg, Wei,
                           Olivia, François, Luca, Arlene, Heather,
                           Guy)

Age group: 3-3.5
Ratio: 1:6
Activity: Free play

Atmosphere: It is a beautiful sunny day and the classroom has been
     heating up with the sun streaming in through the large picture
     windows. Most of the children left with the student educator to
     get a drink from the water fountain. A few of the children stayed
     behind as they seemed very engrossed in their dramatic play.
     Bobby realizes that he is one of the few left behind.

Rationale: Bobby is one of the younger children in the class and
     although his articulation is not at the same level as the other
     children he always expresses his feelings and seems to be able
     to make himself understood. I wonder if his open expression of
     his feelings may help him solve some of the problems he
     encounters during the day.

Observation	Interpretation
Bobby runs to the door and reaches up and grasps the doorknob. He twists it but it does not open; he twists it again and it still does not open. He stands at the door throws his head back and wails, "I'm fustwated; dis door won't open!" He crumbles to the floor and cries for 10 seconds. He stops crying, looks around, sees two boys at the block area and smiles. He wipes his eyes and his cheeks	

with his right shirtsleeve. He sniffles and wipes his nose with his left sleeve. He looks at the wet sleeves, pulls both down over his hands, shakes his arms, and trots off to the block area saying, "Can I play wif you guys?" He stands at the edge of the carpet in the block area looking at the boys. He says, "Dat's a big building. It's great! Wanna put a car near de building?" He pulls a small car out of his pocket. The boy looks up and smiles at him. Bobby moves closer to the boys and falls to his knees beside one of the boys. The boy says, "Okay, put the car here."	

From this running record we can gather information about Bobby's language, social, physical, and emotional skills. These will be discussed later in the section on *Interpretations*.

Exercise 12: Running record

Using a running record format, select one child to watch for a five-minute period in any area of the room. Make that one child the focus of your observation and record everything the child says and does as well as everything that is said to that child and done to the child. For instance, if the child is in the block area piling one block on top of another you would write this information in your observation column. If another child were to enter the block area and brush against your focal child's tower, you would write this down and also record what happened to the tower and how your focal child reacted. Remember to watch for a total of five minutes and jot down everything.

Now set this observation aside and go back to work with the children. When you have a spare moment during the day read what you have recorded over that five-minute observation period. Fill in any gaps in the recording with information that you remember seeing and hearing as the action (verbal and physical) unfolded. To learn more about the child you observed, use a set of different coloured highlighters to underline all of that child's verbalizations (e.g., pink), the child's gross motor actions (e.g., blue), and the child's fine motor actions (e.g., orange). Set this information aside for later reference.

Anecdotal recordings

The anecdotal recording is the most frequently used of the narrative methodologies. It is composed of a short summary of an event that the observer has decided is a very important recording to have on file. An anecdote is a summary of something that the observer has not set out to intentionally record and is usually recorded after it has happened rather than while it is occurring. Consequently, the anecdote is recorded in the past tense and is usually not as graphic in detail as the running record, nor does it tell as much of a story as the running record. However, it does include sufficient detail about the significant behaviour that caught your interest in the first place.

Anecdotal Recording Example 1

Date: April 22, 2006
Time of day: Dismissal time
Number of children: 12
Age group: 4-4.5
Ratio: 1:6
Activity: Dressing for home   (Max)

Atmosphere: It is the end of the day. The children are getting ready to leave for the day and they have spread their outdoor clothes all over the floor space in an attempt to dress themselves.

Rationale: Max usually waits for his mom to dress him. This is the first time that Max has attempted to dress himself.

With a big smile on his face, Max threw his coat onto the floor and dove into the sleeves and flipped the coat over his head. It ended up being upside down with the bottom of the coat around his neck. He continued smiling as he slipped his knapsack on over his coat and ran to sit on the bench with the other children who were already dressed and waiting for their mothers.

Anecdotal Recording Example 2

Date: June 22, 2006
Time of day: Mid afternoon
Number of children: 16
Age group: 4-4.5
Ratio: 1:8
Activity: Outdoor play in the afternoon   (Jenny)

Atmosphere: It was the middle of the afternoon. The weather was
    beautiful and the children were all busy playing outdoors. Jenny
    found a twig and some string and had made herself a bow.
    Jenny had asked for permission to go indoors to get
    "something."

Rationale: Jenny has a wonderful sense of humour that has not been
    easy to record as her comments come so quickly.

    Jenny emerged with a plastic straw that she positioned against
    the string and pulled the straw back against the string. The
    educator said, "Don't you let that go!" Jenny smiled and aimed at
    the educator who said, "If you let that go…" To which Jenny
    responded, "It will be the last straw, eh?"

Anecdotal recordings also include interpretations, which will be
discussed in the *Interpretation* section.

Exercise 13: Anecdotal recording

Using the template presented, record a significant piece of information that you would like to retain because it points out something important about one of the children in your class.

Date:
Time of day:
Number of children:
Age group:
Ratio:
Activity:

Atmosphere:

Rationale:

Anecdote:

Set this anecdote aside to be used later on.

Sampling techniques

Sampling techniques are used for very specific purposes. If you are interested in examining a behavior that does not occur very frequently, but is very important we recommend using *event sampling*.

Event sampling

If properly planned, event sampling can reveal how the behavior began, how it evolved, and how it ended. In order to gather this information you should have a clear idea of the aspects of the behavior that you want to observe and clearly define the behavior in terms of what it looks like when you see it happening.

For example, if you want to study a form of play that sometimes appears to be aggressive but may not actually be you would look at *rough-and-tumble behavior*, and define this behavior as *motor play that overlaps with social play.* It usually takes the form of play fighting "as the children engage in a form of make-believe in which body parts and actions are involved" (Johnson, Christie, & Yawkey; 1999, p. 75). In this form of play the victim and the powerful figure often change roles so that each has a turn being the powerful figure. Examples of verbalizations that accompany rough-and-tumble (R&T) play may include "Pow"; "Bam"; "Fall down 'cuz you're dead." Physical examples of rough-and-tumble play may include *fake punches; chasing; pretend shooting and pretend Karate kicks.* It should be distinguished from real aggressive verbal or physical behaviour. *Verbal aggression is defined as an utterance that is hostile or threatening in tone or a verbal utterance with intent to harm* (e.g., "That is an ugly dress." "No one likes you and you cannot come to my party."). Physical aggression could include a nonverbal act that is hostile in nature and has the intent to harm (e.g., hitting, pinching, biting, kicking, spitting).

Once you have decided on the behavior that will be examined, you create a chart composed of all the relevant factors that you want to include in the recording. For example, in order to differentiate between rough-and-tumble play and an aggressive act you may want to know (a) who was the initiator, (b) the type of behaviour displayed (e.g., rough and tumble play or aggressive behavior) (c) whether it was verbal or non-verbal behaviour, (d) the target of the behaviour, and (e) the type of response the target displayed to the behaviour. The trigger for you to begin filling in the chart is the display of the defined behavior (e.g., rough-and-tumble play or aggressive behaviour).

To gather the information you begin by focusing on a specific child and as soon as the child is involved in a rough-and-tumble or aggressive event, either as the initiator or the target, you begin recording by filling in the columns with the relevant information. If the event does not end after a single initiation and response, you could move to the next line and enter the next sequence of behaviours in the appropriate columns.

Refer to event sampling example found on the following page.

This recording of a sequence of behaviors that begins with a rough-and-tumble initiation by Sam (i.e., "Pow, you're dead.") is entered along the same line with his rough-and-tumble non-verbal behaviour (i.e., Points Lego stick). The name of the target (Bob) is also entered on the same line along with Bob's responses to the rough-and-tumble initiation by Sam. Entering the behaviours along one line gives you a condensed and complete picture of the event. If the rough-and-tumble interaction continues, then you can enter the information from the second sequence as you did for the first and mark the events as they occur.

Date: Nov. 22, 2006

Time of day: Noon

Number of children: 20

Age group: 4.5-5

Ratio: 1:10

Activity: Free Play   (Sam, Bob)

Atmosphere: The weather has been awful – cold and stormy, so the children have not been able to go outdoors for the past three days. It is free-play time and several boys are playing together building Lego structures. A great deal of loud talk is coming from the block area where Sam and Bob are two of the four boys building towers. They are active children and yesterday there were a couple of outbursts between them that included trading punches.

Rationale: Sam and Bob frequently engage in very active play accompanied by verbal exchanges that sound like aggressive interactions. On the surface, they seem to be interested in testing each other's strength and challenging each other about who is the stronger, more powerful character. However, they also seem to be close friends as they always choose one another to engage in this active form of play. It is time to examine whether their play is aggressive (i.e., intent to harm), who is the initiator in these interactions, and where in the room this behaviour usually occurs. Other issues that might be interesting to explore are: (a) the kind of vocabulary they use and (b) if there is anything positive about their exchanges (social issues).

Initiator	Initiations				Target	Responses				Location
	R & T Verbal	R & T Nonverbal	Aggressive Verbal	Aggressive Nonverbal		R & T Verbal	R & T Nonverbal	Aggressive Verbal	Aggressive Nonverbal	
1. Sam	"Pow. You're dead"	Points Lego stick			Bob	"Naw, your gun has no special powers so it missed me. Nah, nah, nah, nah."	Smiles and sticks out tongue and wags tongue.			Block area
2. Bob	"I'm gonna' kill ya' with my super power fist."	Runs at Sam with arm outstretched with hand in a fist			Sam	"I'm invincible so nothing can kill me."	Ducks down. Rolls on floor. Leaps up smiling			Block area
3. Sam	"I'm fast, I'm slippery, and I'm stronger than you."	Grabs Bob by his shirt			Bob	"Can't hold me. Can't hold me" (in sing song voice).	Pulls away smiling and dances backwards away from Sam.			From block area into the main part of the room

Exercise 14: Event sampling

In order to practice the event sampling techniques, it might be best to try to use the grid presented above and record precisely the same kinds of behaviours –that is, rough-and-tumble play and aggressive verbal and/or non-verbal behaviour on the part of a child with a classmate. For this exercise you might select a child in your class who seems to you to be more frequently involved in loud social interactions. Observe that child during a free play period when he/she is more likely to be further away from your watchful eye and may engage in this type of play. Try to use the grid as designed and determine whether or not it works for the purpose of recording acts of rough-and-tumble play or aggression. Record this information over the free play period and then review your findings.

Once you have reviewed the entries look to see if you are surprised by the kind of information you have recorded. Is it possible that the behaviour you thought was aggressive was actually rough-and-tumble play? Remember that most socially adept children do not have any trouble recognizing the difference between rough-and-tumble play and aggressive behaviour.

Interpreting observations

Interpretations are an essential aspect of the observational methodology. When you record the actual observation, you are providing yourself with information that you can work on to help you understand many things about the classroom environment and the children. For example, having observed frequent events of aggressive behaviour displayed by Sam and James in the block area, you may begin to consider the arrangement of the block area as well as their social skills as the possible reasons for their aggressive behaviour. The observational data you have gathered provide the starting point for the real work that you should do with the observations. It is essential to read and reflect on the observational information before you record your interpretations of the child's behaviour. Once you have given careful consideration to what you have observed, you will have to decide what it means in terms of the plans you should make to support various domains of the children's development.

The organizational set-up presented below in the boxed example will provide you with sufficient space to jot down interpretations of the actions and verbalizations you have recorded. As you cannot be certain about the reasons for the child's behavior and can only surmise as to what they may be, your interpretations should reflect this uncertainty. Therefore, the most appropriate words to use are "seems to be," "appears to be," "perhaps," or "might." The sample running record will be used to demonstrate how you might interpret the observational data.

Running Record Example

<u>Date</u>: May 22, 2006
<u>Time of day</u>: Morning
<u>Number of children</u>: 12
<u>Age group</u>: 3-3.5
<u>Ratio</u>: 1:6
<u>Activity</u>: Free play   (Bobby)

<u>Atmosphere</u>: It is a beautiful sunny day and the classroom has been heating up with the sun streaming in through the large picture windows. Most of the children left with the student educator to get a drink from the water fountain. A few of the children stayed behind as they seemed to be very engrossed in their dramatic play. Bobby realizes that he is one of the few left behind.

<u>Rationale</u>: Bobby is one of the younger children in the class and although his articulation is not at the same level as the other children he always expresses his feelings and seems to be able to make himself understood. His open expression of his feelings may help him solve some of the problems he encounters during the day.

Observation	Interpretation
Bobby runs to the door and reaches up and grasps the doorknob. He twists it but it does not open; he twists it again and it still does not open.	Appears to have realized that the majority of his peers are elsewhere and seems to be trying to solve the problem of having been left behind. Seems to have some gross motor or physical strength problems.
He stands at the door throws his head back and wails, "I'm fustwated; dis door won't open!"	Appears to be aware of his emotions and is able to apply an appropriate label.
He crumbles to the floor and cries for 10 seconds.	Seems to express his frustration by crying.

He stops crying, looks around, sees two boys at the block area and smiles. He wipes his eyes and his cheeks with his right shirtsleeve. He sniffles and wipes his nose with his left sleeve. He looks at the wet sleeves, pulls both down over his hands, shakes his arms, and trots off to the block area saying, "Can I play wif you guys?"	Seems to suddenly have become aware of the other children still in the class and appears to be taking care of himself after his crying bout. Appears to be getting ready for a possible interaction with the boys who are in the classroom. Seems to be aware of the social etiquette of asking permission before entering an ongoing group.
He stands at the edge of the carpet in the block area looking at the boys. He says, "Dat's a big building. It's great! Wanna put a car near de building? He pulls a small car out of his pocket. The boy looks up and smiles at him.	Appears to be trying both verbally and physically to be accepted by the boys who are already playing.
Bobby moves closer to the boys and falls to his knees beside one of the boys. The boy says, "Okay, put the car here.	Seems to know how to get himself into the existing group to join the ongoing play.

The interpretations entered in this observational recording tend to focus on Bobby's awareness of his social situation, his emotions, his problem solving skills, and his social skills. Bobby's educator has applied her knowledge of children's social skill development to interpret much of what was observed. The interpretations indicate that the educator has determined that Bobby can take some appropriate action to try to resolve a problem he has encountered. The educator also sees that Bobby can label his emotions even in a stressful situation and can calm himself after exhibiting distress.

The educator has also noted that Bobby possesses the social skills needed to gain entry into an already established playgroup. With this kind of information, the educator can plan to observe other aspects of his development and has learned that Bobby may be a good model for other children in the class who have difficulty entering an already established play group.

It is important to remember that interpretations are inferences that are based upon your recorded observations and as such they are influenced by your own personal lens. Your past experiences, values and beliefs, culture, gender, and education may all have an impact on how you interpret the behaviours you have observed. For example, you may be annoyed with Bobby for not responding quickly enough in the first place so that he could have left the classroom with everyone else. Consequently, you might focus more on his attempts to leave the classroom after everyone else had already left and his subsequent crying than on his ability to label his feelings. This might lead you to interpret his behaviour as evidence of immaturity in that he was unable to make up his mind about what he wanted to do and he was unable to turn the doorknob to open the door and join his peers at the water fountain. A good rule of thumb to follow when interpreting observations is to think in terms of your knowledge of child development and appreciate the skills each child displays. This should lead you to make interpretations that will help you decide how to scaffold each child's learning and development in terms of interactions, materials, equipment, environmental design, and curriculum planning.

Interpretations are essential in following up on detailed observations because they allow you to formulate understandings of children's actions and work and find new meaning in your own work and teaching. That is, everyday moments begin to take on deeper meanings, because you are better able to see the value of what learners do and begin to understand how to build upon their existing competencies, capabilities, and interests. You may then use this information to help children explore and construct new knowledge through interactive and meaningful ways that build upon what they know and how they learn. Your interpretations of observations can also help you to understand how to create meaningful experiences for the children and share this knowledge with the important people in the children's lives.

Exercise 15: Interpreting anecdotal recordings

a) Using information covered in the section "Interpreting observations," write out your interpretations of the following two anecdotal recordings.

Anecdotal Recording Example 1

Date: April 22, 2006
Time of day: Dismissal time
Number of children: 12
Age group: 4-4.5
Ratio: 1:6
Activity: Dressing for home   (Max)

Atmosphere: It is the end of the day. The children are all getting ready to leave for the day and they have spread their outdoor clothes all over the floor space in an attempt to dress themselves.

Rationale: Max usually waits for his mom to dress him. This is the first time that Max has attempted to dress himself.

With a big smile on his face, Max threw his coat onto the floor and dove into the sleeves and flipped the coat over his head. It ended up being upside down with the bottom of the coat around his neck. He continued smiling as he slipped his knapsack on over his coat and ran to sit on the bench with the other children who were already dressed and waiting for their mothers.

Your Interpretation

In order to help you make interpretations, consider the following:

- What did you learn about what Max has taught himself?
- What did you learn about his emotional state when tending to his own needs?
- What did you learn about his spatial skills?

Anecdotal Recording Example 2

> Date: June 22, 2006
> Time of day: Mid afternoon
> Number of children: 16
> Age group: 4-4.5
> Ratio: 1:8
> Activity: Outdoor play in the afternoon   (Jenny)
>
> Atmosphere: It was the middle of the afternoon. The weather was
>   beautiful and the children were all busy playing outdoors. Jenny
>   found a twig and some string and had made herself a bow.
>   Jenny had asked for permission to go indoors to get
>   "something."
>
> Rationale: Jenny has a wonderful sense of humour that has not been
>   easy to record as her comments come so quickly.
>
>
> Jenny emerged with a plastic straw that she positioned against
> the string and pulled the straw back against the string. The
> educator said, "Don't you let that go!" Jenny smiled and aimed at
> the educator who said, "If you let that go…" To which Jenny
> responded, "It will be the last straw, eh?"

Your interpretation

In order to help you make interpretations, consider the following:
- What did you learn about Jenny's language skills?
- What did you learn about her sense of humour?
- What did you learn about her physical skills?

Interpreting the event sampling

Turn to the previous Event Sampling Grid and read the following interpretations of the information provided in the grid.

As Event Sampling uses a different format for recording, we want to show you how you might interpret the information that was gathered. For the event sampling of rough-and-tumble play it is possible to use a paragraph format to address each entry or event that was recorded on the grid. Usually we consider who initiated the behaviour, the kind of initiation (e.g., verbal or nonverbal), the target of the initiation, the type of response (e.g., verbal or nonverbal), where in the room it occurred, and what it was all about. It could be that the type of play the children engaged in during the observation occurs consistently in the same area of the room. If this is the case, then it would be important to examine that area for particular elements such as the: (a) amount of space in the area; (b) number of children in the area; (c) particular children playing in the area; (d) type of materials present; (e) number of items available to the children; (f) location of the area with respect to ease of supervision. See below for the interpretation of the event sampling.

In this observation the first issue to note is that the children's behaviour was categorized as rough-and-tumble play and not aggressive behaviour. While the verbal initiations showed evidence of what could be seen as aggression, from the context of the play and the tone indicated, the behaviour was playful without evidence of intent to harm. It is interesting to note that the participants were two boys and rough-and-tumble play usually involves boys rather than girls. Sam was the initiator twice whereas Bob did so once. The kind of initiations recorded were combinations of verbal and nonverbal behaviour for each child. If you focus on the words used you will see that there are sounds that are typical of rough-and-tumble play (e.g., Pow), threats of destruction, and statements of comparative strength. In terms of nonverbal displays of behaviour, if these behaviours had been displayed in another context and the words were spoken in another tone, we would have categorized the behaviour as aggressive because of the outstretched fist and the grabbing of the shirt. However, considering the context, this appears to be play fighting rather than real fighting. The reference to special powers and invincibility verbalized by the target (i.e., Bob) should confirm the interpretation of this event as rough-and-tumble play. Bob's nonverbal response that involved smiling and mild taunting (e.g., sticks out tongue and wags tongue) indicates that he is reading Sam's initiation as rough-and-tumble play. The fact that this play continues in this manner also tells us that the boys are accustomed to this type of play and this is confirmed by the fact that even when they touch one another, the play remains at the rough-and-tumble level. From this interaction we can interpret something about their social skills as well. While Sam initiated this type of play, Bob was able to read it accurately, maintain the play in this manner, and not raise the stakes. From their verbal exchanges we can see something of their receptive vocabulary (e.g., invincible), their comprehension of the term, and their reasoning (e.g., "I'm invincible so nothing can kill me").

As far as the environment is concerned, each exchange happened in the block area where they were building. We know that children are tempted by the characteristics of Lego to construct more than buildings; guns are almost inevitable. But we also see that although four boys were constructing in the area only two (Sam and Bob) actually engaged in rough-and-tumble play. We will have to watch their interactions more closely and for more than one day to determine why their construction play transforms into rough-and-tumble play and the point at which this occurs. We will note if this rough-and-tumble play occurs well into the construction time (as we could reason this form of play may occur when they are tired of the construction play, or we might question whether there are sufficient Lego blocks to support complex construction and if not, that might be the trigger for rough-and–tumble play.

As you can see, there is much that can be determined from observing an event and while the initial observation may generate more questions than answers, it can provide important clues that may lead you to the answers.

Exercise 16: Interpreting your running record

Use your five-minute running record to practice writing interpretations. Create a column for interpretations to the right of your column for the observed behaviours and try to enter an interpretation for each of the behaviours observed over the five-minute period.

<u>Date</u>:
<u>Time of day</u>:
<u>Number of children</u>:
<u>Age group</u>:
<u>Ratio</u>:
<u>Activity</u>:
<u>Atmosphere:</u>
<u>Rationale:</u>

Observation	Interpretation

Exercise 17: Interpreting your anecdotal recording

Using your anecdotal recording add an interpretation to complete the information required for an anecdotal recording.

Date:
Time of day:
Number of children:
Age group:
Ratio:
Activity:
Classroom atmosphere:
Rationale:
Recorded observation:
Interpretation:

Exercise 18: Interpreting your event sampling

In order to interpret the event sampling of rough-and-tumble play behaviour you recorded, you could use a paragraph format to address each entry or event as it occurred. You might consider the following event sampling points:

1. Where in the room the event occurred;

2. Amount of space in the area;

3. Number of children in the area;

4. Particular children playing in the area;

5. Type of materials present;

6. Number of items available to the children;

7. Who initiated the event;

8. What it was all about.

The following exercises are designed to utilize your new knowledge about curriculum and observations. In order to do these exercises successfully we recommend that you review the corresponding curriculum sections and keep them close at hand.

Exercise 19: Using observations to design the physical environment and support classroom organization

a) Consider your physical classroom environment and over a 2- or 3-day period, record observations of how children utilize the space during free play. You might use a running record to record the information initially and then transfer the information to a grid like the one presented below. This will be helpful to do an assessment of the classroom environment

In writing your recordings remember the following:

1. Be accurate in your recording.

2. Use objective language that is a full description of what you are observing.

3. Try not to miss important parts of the sequence of events.

4. Record only what actually happens while you are observing.

5. Include basic information that is important to know for every observation recorded.

In order to gather the information needed to answer the questions posed below you may wish to include a detailed diagram of the classroom set up to help you determine where and when to look at what is happening within the classroom.

b) Select an area to observe. Plan to record the activity in the area for a 5-minute block of time. Begin by recording the names of all the children in the area. Then take one minute to scan the area and specify what each child is doing including what materials each child is using. Do this systematically five times within the 5-minute period. Set the recording sheet aside and make sure that all is well with the children. Select a second area to study and repeat the procedure. Repeat this format until all of the areas in the room have been examined over a two- to three-day period. Each day find time to review your recordings and fill in any gaps in the recording that may seem apparent and for which you have a clear recollection of what transpired. Then you can use the grid below to fill in the information in each column.

Time	Centre being observed	Names of children in the centre	Materials being used	Children's activities	Evidence of learning

c) After you have collected your observations, you may use the chart below to provide you with more information.

Classroom space used most frequently	Classroom space used least frequently
Which centers or areas were used most often?	Which centers or areas did you observe to be used the least?
Select one of these centers to examine in greater depth. _____ Describe the centre. Measure the amount of space available, list the selection of materials, and describe the arrangement, organization, and accessibility of materials.	Select one of these centers to examine in greater depth. _____ Describe the centre. Measure the amount of space available, list the selection of materials, and describe the arrangement, organization, and accessibility of materials.
In this centre, did the children engage in solitary, parallel, or group play?	In this centre, did the children engage in solitary, parallel, or group play?
Were the children using the available materials?	Were the children using the available materials?

Classroom space used most frequently	Classroom space used least frequently
What kind of learning did you observe happening in this centre with the materials available? For example, did you observe children's language, cognitive, social-emotional, or fine and gross motor development?	What kind of learning did you observe happening in this centre with the materials available? For example, did you observe children's language, cognitive, social-emotional, or fine and gross motor development? Based on your observations of the least frequently used center, what changes could you make to this center (e.g., new materials, different organization, more space)? How could you involve the children in making these changes?

Exercise 20: Opportunities for exploration and learning in outdoor settings

Record observations of children as they enter the playground over a two- or three-day period. You may use either running record or anecdotal recording techniques to record your observations. Concentrate on what parts of the playground the children go to, what equipment they choose to play with, and the kind of play they engage in (e.g., solitary, parallel or group).

Do not forget to also include "Information about children and playground," "playground atmosphere," and "rationale" as part of your recordings.

Include interpretations of your recordings.

When you have completed your recordings of the observations and interpretations, review the information and see if you can answer the following questions.

1. How is the playground arranged to encourage children to engage in various activities in different areas of the playground? Does the space encourage children to engage in independent hands-on learning experiences either by themselves or with their peers? If yes, how does it do so?

2. What did you learn about children's interests through these observations?

3. What did you learn about children's existing competencies through these observations?

4. What did you learn about children's individual learning and play styles through these observations?

5. What did you learn about how the playground is arranged so that children have some privacy or can play in dyads or groups?

6. Does the playground appear to appeal to a diverse group of children with various interests, competencies, and learning styles?

7. Did you observe children sharing ideas and learning together through exploration and discovery? What exactly did they do?

Based on your review of your observations, consider changes you would make to the outdoor environment to support and extend children's learning.

What changes would you make to the outdoor environment to encourage children to engage in independent hands-on learning experiences either alone or with other children?

What equipment would you add to the playground to extend their interests and emerging competencies?

Exercise 21: Taking initiative and making choices

In order to prepare yourself to carry out this exercise review the information about taking initiative and making choices found in the Curriculum section, as well as the event sampling information found in the Observation section.

To incorporate children's interests into the program it is important to create opportunities that allow children, as well as you, the educator, to take initiative and make choices in the classroom. Recording observations of when children and educators take initiative and make choices, how the process evolves, and the result of the process will provide you with valuable information for curriculum development.

a) Using the event sampling technique, begin with a clear idea of the aspects of the behavior that you want to observe and define the behavior in terms of what it looks like when you see it happening. For example, you might define child initiative-taking and making choices as when a child states, "I want to paint now." or "Could we stay inside and play some more with the pirate ship and go outside later?" or when two children bring the plates and cups from the house centre to the block centre. Examples of educator initiative-taking and making choices may include: "We need to write a get well letter to Jennifer because she is still sick" or "It is snack time Bobby, could you pour the milk?" or "Put your boots on now, we are going outside" or "Let's read *Where the Wild Things Are*."

To help you gather observations and determine when and how often you, as the educator, and the children take initiative and make choices, create a grid similar to the one provided for you in the event sampling example. However, this new grid will correspond to the aspects of initiative-taking and making choices. Use the grid to gather observations during a 2-hour time frame (e.g., 9:00 – 11:00).

b) Reflect upon the information you have recorded and consider the following questions. You may wish to respond in the space provided or write your responses in your journal.

How many times did you take initiative or make choices in the classroom during the 2-hour time frame?

How many times did children take initiative or make choices in the classroom during the 2-hour time frame?

To calculate the proportion of teacher initiations versus the proportion of child initiations you will need to add the number of times children took initiative or made choices plus the number of times you took initiative or made choices to establish the total number of initiations in the classroom over the 2-hour period.
What was the total number of initiations (teacher + child)?

It is important to look at the proportion of teacher initiations versus child initiations to make sense of the information. So divide the number of teacher-initiations by the total number of initiations that you have observed.
For example, if you observed 15 teacher-initiations and 10 child-initiations, you would calculate 15 ÷(15+10) = .60. That means that 60% of the initiations are made by the teacher.

What is the proportion of teacher initiations versus child initiations for the time you observed?

Did the proportion of teacher initiations surprise you in any way?

c) Now, take a moment to reflect upon the proportion of initiations you made versus the proportion of initiations the children made in combination with the additional observations you gathered.

If the proportion of initiations you made versus the proportion of initiations the children made surprised you because it yielded a higher number in favour of initiations you made, consider the following:

- the purpose of your initiations (e.g., to give direction *"Let's put our coats on to go outside."*; to make choices *"Emily is sick at home. What can we do to help her feel better?"*; to provide information *"Allan and Jenny are not here today."*).
- the context in which they occurred (e.g., in block area, at lunch time, getting ready to go outdoors).
- the children's responses to your initiations (e.g., the children ignored you by continuing to play when you said, *"It's time to clean up the trucks"*; the children required redirection when they came to the snack table without washing their hands and you said *"Please remember to wash your hands before snack."*).

Now that you have reflected upon these elements, consider whether there were times when you could have encouraged the children to take initiative, make some decisions on their own, or share the responsibility with you rather than assuming the responsibility yourself? In order to encourage children to take more initiative and make choices, it may be necessary to provide them with some information, and to encourage them to participate in decision-making and generating input. The degree of decision-making in which they can participate and the amount of input they can provide will depend on the individual classroom situation. Your goal as an educator should be to influence classroom situations and interactions in order to maximize children's decision-making opportunities. For the following classroom situations:

- rather than saying *"Let's put our coats on to go outside,"* consider what information you could provide for the children and still encourage them to decide what they need to put on in order to go outside?
- rather than saying *"We should make a card for Emily because she is at home sick,"* consider what information you could offer the children that would encourage them to make decisions about how to respond to their classmate who has been at home sick for a few days.
- rather than saying *"Allan and Jenny are not here today,"* consider what you might say in order to help the children take the initiative required to notice who is absent.

If the proportion of initiations you made versus the proportion of initiations the children made yielded a number that was equal, or in favour of child initiations, consider the following:

- the purpose of their initiations (e.g., to give you information "*I saw a big truck on the way to day care. It made a lot of noise and was really cool!*"; to show interest, for example while you are stapling children's art work to put into their files several children ask questions about the stapler and how it works; to make their wishes known, for example a child walks by the Lego table that already has four children playing there. Four is the number you have determined to be the maximum for that table, and the child says, "*I want to play here.*").
- the context in which their initiations occurred (e.g., block area, lunch time, getting ready to go outdoors).
- your response to their initiations (e.g., you agreed by saying, "*That sounds like a good idea.*"; you did not support their request to paint by saying, "*We're not using the paint today, but we will tomorrow.*"

Now consider how you could build on the children's initiations and decision-making and incorporate them into the curriculum. In order to do this it is important to use observations to help you identify children's points-of-interest, and to engage the children in generating possibilities of how these points-of-interest can be included in the curriculum. For the following classroom situations:

- when a child informs you by saying, "*I saw a big truck on the way to day care. It made a lot of noise and was really cool!*", consider how you could integrate his/her interest in trucks into the curriculum. Consider what you might say to the child, what materials you might add to the classroom, how you could encourage other children to participate in the child's interest in trucks, and how you could extend the activity over several days?
- when the children show an interest in the stapler you are using, consider how you could incorporate this interest into the curriculum. What you might say to help them generate ideas that would provide them with opportunities to use the stapler, experiment with a variety of materials, and use the stapler in different types of activities.
- when a child indicates that she would like to work in a particular area of the classroom, even if that area appears to be full, consider how you could engage the child in solving this problem. Consider what you might say to encourage the child to contemplate ideas that would result in her joining the other children in that area, and what environmental changes may be required to make this happen.

Documentation

Documentation is the fourth pathway that guides you in developing classroom strategies that reflect a constructivist curriculum framework. Documentation may take many shapes and forms. Drawings by children, samples of their work, photographs, written language entries dictated by the children and/or your own written entries, and objects the children deem to be important in representing their experiences are all examples of documentation. Documentation always includes descriptions and interpretations of children's learning as this helps members of the learning community to recognize and understand the children's experiences and the growth of their knowledge. Documentation can take the form of a panel that consists of photographs that are accompanied by your descriptions and analysis of what the children are doing (see examples in the section of pictures in the manual). These photographs are meant to capture examples of children's understanding and learning. On the other hand, documentation can record the work of an individual child (e.g., three-dimensional creations, a photograph of a complex roadway built in the sand table, a drawing by the child of a recipe for making a fruit salad).

Through the documentation process, you create a history of classroom experiences that can be revisited and extended. Documentation offers a visual image and a written record of children's prior learning. This provides the foundation to help you create new opportunities for meaningful and relevant learning experiences for children. It also allows you to communicate with others regarding the nature and value of children's work, providing clear evidence of the growth and development of children's learning over time.

To successfully utilize documentation in a constructivist curriculum framework, it is important to consider it from the following perspectives: (a) the role of documentation in early childhood settings, (b) the strategies used to create documentation in early childhood classrooms, and (c) the documentation of your learning process.

Role of documentation in early childhood classrooms

- Documentation provides opportunities for you and the children to discuss classroom experiences, thereby sharing ideas and allowing you to become co-constructors of classroom knowledge.

It is a way to build upon children's previous experiences and design meaningful and relevant learning opportunities. Documentation provides a natural bridge that connects children's experiences to current activities and discussion. For example, as you interact with children in the house area and they engage in a discussion of how to make muffins, you may relate their discussion to a previous class experience of visiting a bakery. You may refer them to a documentation panel that you jointly constructed of that visit that may allow them to recall the visit in more detail, thereby increasing their contribution to the discussion. The discussion may result in your adding equipment and materials such as muffin tins and baker's hats to the play area. Further, it may serve as a spontaneous activity in which you and the children make muffins for snack.

- Documentation is a source and an inspiration for curriculum design and implementation by you and by the children.

Documentation facilitates the creation of opportunities that emerge from previous classroom experiences and that build on and strengthen children's learning. Documentation panels that use relevant and meaningful photographs or drawings to preserve classroom experiences make it easier for you and the children to recall and to use those experiences as a source for new learning possibilities. For example, you may have a documentation panel in your classroom that represents a recent class field trip to buy pumpkins at the market. You may observe a few of the children showing an interest in the panel as they point to the pictures and begin discussing whose pumpkin was the heaviest. They may hypothesize several ways of figuring out the weight of the pumpkins. One child suggests that the biggest one is always the heaviest, while another insists that the round pumpkins are the heaviest. This interaction may give you the idea of adding weigh scales and pumpkins of different shapes and sizes to the classroom for children to explore the concept of weight and size.

- Documentation provides evidence of children's growth and development of learning over time.

By documenting children's work and accomplishments (e.g., several pieces of art accumulated over time), you have concrete evidence of their progress. By recording the date on the documentation, you can track how the complexity of children's learning processes have evolved and changed over time.

- Documentation presents children with evidence that their learning endeavors and work are valued and respected by you and by the wider community. This leads to an enhanced sense of pride and accomplishment in their work.

Children are naturally very invested in the work that they are engaged in and proud of their accomplishments. By being surrounded by representations of their experiences that include their language and ideas, they are reminded that their work is important to you and to all members of their learning community.

- Documentation creates opportunities to communicate with others regarding the nature and value of children's work.

As you document classroom experiences that you and the children have engaged in, you facilitate others' recognition and appreciation of those experiences as learning opportunities. For example, parents may communicate their concern that children in your classroom are not learning anything but are simply playing. Through a documentation panel of children engaged in making play dough that includes photographs, children's drawings, your observations, and your interpretations of the children's experiences as they made the play dough, you highlight the note-worthy learning experiences of measuring, hypothesizing, and representing their understanding. You illustrate that as children make predictions, they consider and express possibilities that develop their language and cognitive skills. As they combine materials and solve problems, children develop math skills and strengthen communication and negotiation skills. Through the documentation panel, you may educate parents regarding the nature and value of children's work.

Strategies for creating documentation in early childhood classrooms

- ✓ Let your observations of children's interests and activities guide you as to what may be relevant for documenting.

- ✓ Let children's ideas and suggestions lead you to create the documentation, what is represented, and how it is described.

- ✓ Include a variety of representations such as drawings by the children, samples of their work, photographs, words recorded by you or the children, three-dimensional creations, or objects collected by the children.

- ✓ Include representations of actual experiences and events (e.g., photographs of field trips to the market or the local park).

- ✓ Include representations of children's predictions, interpretations, and hypotheses (i.e., their ideas of what might happen or develop as a result of certain situations).

- ✓ Present individual representations created by one child or many children.

✓ Create panels made up of various representations arranged to tell a story, which may use one type of representation (e.g., photographs) or a variety of types of representations (e.g., photographs, children's drawings, and three-dimensional creations).

✓ Include descriptions dictated by children that are recorded by you or the children.

✓ Include recordings of your observations and interpretations of children's learning.

The shape and form of your documentation may depend on one of the following:

- Children's interests

In order for learning to be meaningful and relevant, it is important to allow children to guide the shape and form of the documentation process. For example, children in your setting may be more interested in representing their ideas through drawings and photographs than in dictating stories or writing stories. It is important to support their interests while slowly introducing other types of representations that may be used to complement and enhance their original interests.

- Administrative requirements

As your classroom may be part of a larger centre, you may find that your choice of the shape and form of documentation may be influenced by the administrative requirements of your organization. For example, you may be in a setting where taking photographs of children is prohibited due to matters of security and confidentiality. This does not mean that you cannot engage in the documentation process, but, rather, that you may need to resort to a modified approach whereby you take photographs of the activities without including the children's faces.

- Classroom resources

Access and availability of resources often influence how activities evolve and the shape they take in early childhood classrooms. For example, you may not always have easy access to a variety or an abundance of supplies to support documentation. As a result, you may have to advocate strongly to purchase a camera, a memory stick, or a printer to allow you to carry out this very important aspect of your program. Or, you may consider approaching parents or local businesses for donations or organizing a fund-raising activity that will help you purchase the supplies you need to support documentation activities.

Simple Documentation

Documentation as a support
to classroom routines.

Documentation as a support to
language and literacy.

Documentation as a way to communicate
information with children.

Types of Documentation Panels

Panel created by children
with adult help.

Using photographs and children's
dictations to tell a story.

Representing children's thoughts
and sharing with all.

Three dimensional panel invites
interest from many.

Using Documentation To Tell A Story

"Tell me about the rocket..."   "And then the bridge..."

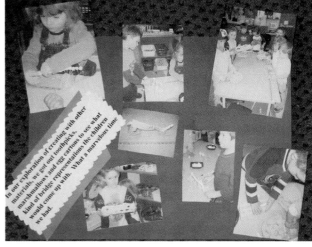

On Making This Rocket

Created by Jeremy & Brendan
Painted by Christopher, Breanna & a lot of others

Chris: Tell me about the rocket.
Jeremy: This is the exhaust pipe, it protects ...we had to tape on it to make it not fall down. These are wings, this thing makes the whole thing wobble.'
Chris: What is it's name?
Jeremy: Tooth. That thing holds on to the exhaust pipe and make it not leak. These are more wings in case it falls. It has exterior pipes so it won't fall.

Chris: What can you tell me about the rocket?
Brendan: Well, I can tell you how we made it. Jeremy made the first part, I came along and cut these triangles and then I helped him tape this part on. We put this on. I think we made this made this part. I think Jeremy put these on. And then we painted it. Jeremy and then a lot of other people and Jeremy and me and a lot of other people.

Chris: What did you paint?
Christopher: I painted blue for a couple minutes and I painted purple.

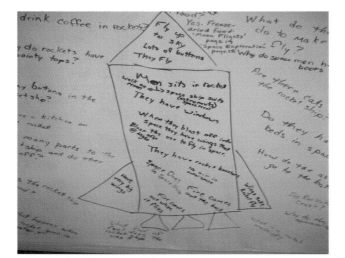

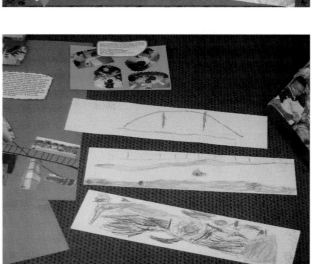

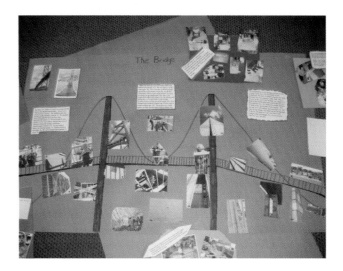

Documentation As Support To Emerging Artists

These well known, world renound artists used hand-held mirrors to observe their reflections before creating these amazing, one-of-a-kind <u>self portraits</u>. They chose a variety of mediums to create these masterpieces, such as, pastels and water-colours. The artists would like to thank you for visiting their art Gallery and encourage you to look around and find photographs of them during their creative process.

Thank you.
from the Management at Point Pleasant Gallery

Documenting your own learning process — a personal portfolio

While documentation plays a significant role in assisting you to create meaningful learning experiences for the children in your classroom, it may also prove to be a valuable tool for recording and reviewing your own learning as you strengthen your understanding of constructivism. Through documentation you can create a history of your individual learning experiences that you can revisit, reflect upon, and extend in personally meaningful ways.

You may choose to document your learning process by taking photographs, writing journal entries, recording observations, or using any combination of approaches as a means to capture moments that represent salient elements of your classroom experiences. As well, the learning exercises you have been completing throughout this manual may contribute to your documentation as they will provide you with a record of your thoughts, your ideas, and your knowledge about children, curriculum, and constructivism. As well as recording observations and thoughts about your classroom decisions, you may also use documentation of children's learning experiences as a means of connecting your classroom strategies to the principles of constructivism.

The documentation strategy you choose is a personal one and may depend on your comfort level, available resources, available time, and specific situation. By engaging in personal documentation in an organized and consistent manner, you will be able to develop a personal portfolio that will represent the growth and development of your knowledge and your understanding of classroom practices reflective of a constructivist framework.

Exercise 22: Documenting through drawings

This activity is an ongoing one that may be carried out at various times during the day depending on classroom experiences and children's interests.

- As children draw pictures, either individually or as part of a group experience, use an open-ended questioning technique and ask them to tell you about their pictures (e.g., "Tell me about what you are drawing." " Tell me what you have done with the paint to get this combination of colours."). Write down what the children tell you in their own words.

- You may write the information on the drawing, if there is room and if the child agrees.

- Alternatively, you may write the child's story on a separate piece of paper and attach it to the picture.

- Include the date on the drawing or paper. You may wish to put the date on the back of the paper so that you do not interfere with the drawing.

- Ask the child(ren)where you should hang their drawing in the classroom. Once a spot has been chosen, involve the child(ren) in hanging it up. You may also designate a particular section of the wall or a bulletin board that is reserved for these kinds of drawings.

- Over the next couple of days, refer back to the drawings at times when they appear to connect with classroom experiences. For example, if two boys are discussing what pumpkins look like, you may focus their attention on the drawing hanging on the wall that one of the boys produced after he and his parents visited the local farmers' market. You may also focus their attention on the words included on the drawing by saying, "Do you remember what you said about the pumpkin that you drew?" Encourage this kind of interaction so as to contribute to their on-going conversation about pumpkins.

Exercise 23:Documenting trips and outings

In order to carry out this exercise, you will need to plan a trip or outing to explore a part of your community. The destination for your trip should be based on the children's interests and competencies, which you may have determined during your observations and documentation of their learning processes. You will also need a camera, the ability to develop film in a timely manner or to download the pictures onto a computer, and poster board.

Please note, while this exercise centres on documenting during trips and outings, the same process can be followed to document any relevant classroom experience (e.g., interesting constructions in the block corner).

While you are on your trip, observe children's interests and behaviours as they explore materials, make predictions and interpretations, and interact with each other. Take photographs of these occurrences and record anecdotal observations.

When your photographs are developed or downloaded, share them with the children and together create a documentation panel to tell the story of your trip.

In order to complete your documentation panel, remember the following:

> ➢ Let the children's ideas and suggestions lead in the creation of the panel, what is represented, and how it is described.

> ➢ Include descriptions dictated by children that you have recorded.

> ➢ Include recordings of your observations of children's learning.

> ➢ Give children the opportunity to include additional representations on the panel if they wish, for example drawings of the trip or objects that were collected during the outing.

> ➢ Ask the children where they want to hang their panel in the classroom. It may be a good idea to hang it in a place that is easily accessible for the parents to see. Thus, they can use this as an opportunity to talk to their children about the outing.

> ➢ Once the panel has been displayed, use it as the basis for facilitating further discussions and as an opportunity to plan further experiences.

Exercise 24: Documentation as evidence of growth and development of learning over time

In order to carry out this exercise you will need to collect samples of children's work and representations over a period of two or three months. As you collect the samples, make sure you include the following information for each one:

1. The date the sample was collected.

2. Any observations you have recorded that accompany the work sample or representation.

3. Any interpretations of children's learning that you have recorded and that accompany the work sample or representation.

Collectively, these samples of children's work and representations provide you with concrete evidence of their progress over time. They can be used to discuss with parents and colleagues how the complexity of children's learning has changed over time. Consider how the documentation is evidence of children's development across various domains. For example, by reviewing children's drawings over several months you should be able to note or describe the development of their fine motor skills. As another example, the children's ability to understand the concept of size may be evident in their descriptions and photographs of the towers that they have constructed in the block corner. You may want to organize your interpretations according to areas of development or particular skills (e.g., self-help, cutting) that you expect them to have learned.

Reflection

Reflection is the fifth pathway of this manual. As an important element of a constructivist curriculum framework, reflection enables you to consider your practice in an analytical way. Ideas and insights that arise through reflection are essential building blocks that you can use in constructing positive and respectful relationships as well as meaningful curriculum. Reflection may occur privately in a journal or may be shared with colleagues as a way of understanding what has occurred in the classroom setting or on the playground. It provides you with information that will determine how to proceed in fostering positive and meaningful learning experiences for you and the children in your classroom.

- Reflection strengthens your understanding of children's behaviours.

As you record observations of children's behaviours and reflect on those observations through interpretation (as presented in section 3), you gain a greater insight into how children behave and understand the world around them. Taking the time to reflect on observations can help you to determine children's interests, competencies, approaches to learning situations, and reactions to classroom experiences. These reflections contribute to the development of portfolios in which you document aspects of children's learning. These portfolios can then serve as a basis for informed communications between you and the children's parents and you and your colleagues. In addition, the portfolios are helpful in designing relevant and meaningful curriculum strategies.

- Reflection assists you in designing and implementing meaningful curriculum strategies.

As you consider the strategies that you implement in your classroom (as presented in chapter 2), reflection encourages you to consider why you have chosen those strategies, and how they connect with and support children's interests and competencies. For example, reflection plays a vital role in making curriculum decisions (e.g., activities to implement, materials to include, or appropriate field trips). In addition, observing children's reactions to classroom experiences, listening to their discussions, and reflecting on this information is essential in designing and implementing a curriculum that is relevant and meaningful.

- Reflection allows for understanding personal learning.

Your reflections may be documented in a personal journal that chronicles your ideas and insights about children's learning and curriculum, or captured in the interpretation process that accompanies your recorded observations or documentation panels. Reflection strengthens your understanding of children's behaviours and assists you in designing and implementing meaningful curriculum.

- Reflection enables you to consider your values and beliefs and connect them to curriculum strategies consistent with a constructivist framework.

The decisions you make as to where curriculum ideas come from, what direction they take, how they evolve, and how they are represented are all connected to who you are as an educator. Your knowledge about child development, the individual children in your classroom, and the curriculum possibilities also play a role in these decisions. Throughout this manual you have been encouraged to reflect upon and consider your values and beliefs and the ways in which they inspire your views about children, curriculum, and classroom practices. The information and exercises presented have been designed to engage you in a reflective process by focusing on what you do in the classroom. They are meant to help you consider how your decisions are connected with values and beliefs consistent with a constructivist framework.

In continuing this reflective process, it may be helpful to consider the following questions:

1. What were the easy aspects of this process for me?

2. What were the difficult aspects of this process for me?

3. What does this tell me about myself, my views about children, about curriculum, and the classroom decisions I make?

4. What is my next step in continuing to build positive relationships with children and the learning community?

5. Have I noticed evidence of my changing values, beliefs, or classroom practices?

6. What did I learn about the children in my classroom during this process?

7. What did I learn about myself during this process?

Exercise 25: A personal portfolio

In order to carry out this exercise, you will need to collect representations of your own experiences as you have worked through this manual. Some of these may include the following:

1. Learning exercises that accompany the manual and that you have completed.

2. Your learning journal.

3. Classroom photographs.

4. Samples of recorded observations of children and classroom events.

5. Samples of classroom documentation experiences.

6. Samples of learning opportunity experiences that you have implemented.

Organize these representations in chronological order in an album or portfolio.

Review the representations and reflect on them. In doing so, consider the following questions:

- ✓ Which aspects of this process were easy for me?
- ✓ Which aspects of this process were more difficult for me?
- ✓ What does this tell me about myself, my views about children and about curriculum, and my classroom decisions?
- ✓ What could I do next in order to continue to build positive relationships with children and the learning community of which I am a part?
- ✓ Have I noticed evidence of my changing values, beliefs, or classroom practices?

✓ What did I learn about the children in my classroom during this process?

✓ What did I learn about myself during this process?

Conclusion

To conclude our journey we will reflect upon the information we have shared with you. To begin this process we will reiterate our chosen definition of constructivism, and then review the role that is played by values and beliefs, curriculum design, observations, documentation, and reflection in creating a constructivist classroom.

Constructivism defined

Throughout this manual we have referred to constructivism as a theory about knowledge and learning (Fosnot, 2005, p. ix). To that end we have encouraged you to know yourself. As well, we encouraged you to examine the validity of what you think learning is, your understanding of how children learn, and what your role should be in the process.

Values and beliefs

We introduced you to the notion that you have particular values (i.e., deeply held views) and beliefs (i.e., personal convictions) that are the product of your age, gender, past experiences, education, family, and cultural background. We invited you to engage in exercises to help you identify your values and beliefs and decide which of these determine how you interact with the children in your classroom. By engaging in the exercises in this manual we hope that you have developed an awareness of your particular values and beliefs and that you understand that they are the filters through which you see the world and, more particularly, your classroom environment.

The section on values and beliefs was intended to help you see how both factors influence the decisions you make regarding curriculum design, the materials and equipment selected for the classroom, the physical layout of the classroom, and your understanding of the needs and interests of the children in your class. They also determine how you respond to certain situations in your classroom. For example, if you value independence, you may be inclined to buy materials and set up the classroom environment in a manner that facilitates the development of independence (e.g., small pitchers to support children's pouring of milk or juice into their own cups). Your beliefs may come into play when you are faced with a very capable child who wants you to do everything and, for instance, refuses to pour a cup of juice. However, now that you have had an opportunity to reflect upon your beliefs, and have used this manual as a resource for the development of a constructivist classroom philosophy, your decisions may be tempered by your knowledge of child development and your understanding of the needs of that child at that particular moment in time. In using this manual, you have been encouraged to identify your values and beliefs, develop an honest awareness of them, and determine how they have influenced your interactions with the children, as well as your planning and design of the curriculum and the classroom environment.

Curriculum design

Curriculum design occupies a significant portion of this manual because we wanted to take the time to address the important issue of what you do with the children each day and the basis for your decisions. In a constructivist classroom, children acquire knowledge about their physical and social world through active engagement with their environment and by communicating with others. Educators in a constructivist classroom support children's development of knowledge by recognizing their current understanding and using this as a foundation for further learning. The section on curriculum design is divided into two major topic areas. The first is a presentation of a constructivist's view of children as learners, explorers, and constructors of knowledge and understanding, and it includes an exploration of how your values mesh with a constructivist view of children. The second is a discussion and exploration of daily classroom practices that is centered on child development, the design and components of the physical classroom environment, program schedules, educator-planned experiences as learning opportunities, and behaviour guidance. We emphasized these topics as they are important elements that should be considered by an educator in a constructivist classroom. There are several exercises contained in the curriculum section that were designed to encourage you to explore each of the topics and to make the information personally meaningful. We hope that this portion of the manual has caused you to reflect on the kinds of activities you have engaged in with the children, the rationale for doing these activities (e.g., child development issues), and the outcomes of the experiences for you and the children as co-constructors of knowledge and understanding. We understand that changing the source of curriculum decisions from you, the educator, as sole designer to a design partnership between you *and* the children can be a challenge. However, our experiences have taught us that it is a worthwhile challenge that creates an environment in which everyone learns valuable information from one another.

You will note that in this section we have used the term *behaviour guidance* rather than *discipline* or *behaviour management.* The term guidance is reflective of a constructivist philosophy in which the development and practice of self-regulation, self-respect, and empathy towards others is very important. An educator can help to instill these characteristics through the creation of a positive learning environment in which the child learns about positive and negative emotions and develops an understanding of what is socially acceptable, and how to solve social problems. Here we must emphasize the point that success in the area of behaviour guidance requires knowledge and understanding of child development.

Observations

In order to provide an environment in which constructivism can flourish, the educator must know what is happening with every child in the classroom so that each child can be engaged in meaningful and appropriate ways. To be so informed, the educator must gather relevant data while the class is in session and the children are engaged in various activities both indoors and outdoors. To accomplish this task requires the development of observational skills. In the chapter on observations we encouraged you to explore the various techniques that should enable you to see with accuracy what the children in your class are doing, how to record this information, and how to interpret what you observed. More specifically, we shared with you the concept that observations allow you to accumulate information about the skills, interests, and needs of individual children or groups of children in your classroom. The value of observing, recording, and interpreting situations lies in the gathering of relevant data about various aspects of your classroom environment.

Observations enable you to see how your classroom environment is used by the children, and can help you determine what changes or additions should be made to enrich the children's experiences and opportunities for learning. This kind of information is essential to determine how to plan appropriate, stimulating, and meaningful activities that address and support children's needs and interests in a constructivist classroom.

We have tried to walk you through the development of observational skills that are relevant for preschool settings. The most basic of techniques is the running record and we encouraged you to use this technique in any situation in which you want to assess what the children are doing in order to learn more about their social, emotional, language, cognitive, and physical skills. Anecdotal recordings are even easier to perform because they are short recordings of pieces of information that relate to a very specific issue that you wish to document, such as a child's sense of humour or a child's creative use of language. This manual also introduced you to one of the more interesting sampling techniques--event sampling--so that you would have the skills required to record important issues associated with events such as the initiation of interactions, the display of aggression or prosocial behaviours, or the display of problem-solving skills.

Following the explanation of the various techniques useful for recording observations, we included information about interpreting your findings. The purpose of interpretation is to help you, the observer, reflect upon what you saw in order to understand more clearly the reasons for the child's behaviour (i.e., actions and verbalizations). The special language used in interpretations (e.g., appears to, seems to) acknowledges our recognition of the fact that we do not know with certainty why the child did or said particular things. We must base our interpretations on what we know about child development and the likelihood of the child's motivations for behaving in a particular manner.

We organized the exercises in this manual to show you how you can learn everything you need to know about the children and the environment by spending time observing the children and recording how they use the environment. Although these exercises may have been time-consuming initially, the more frequently you engage in observing and recording, the less taxing the process will be and the more important observational data will become for your curriculum decisions. We hope that by completing the observational exercises you have learned a great deal about the children in your class, the knowledge they have, the kind of activities they are interested in, and the most appropriate way to support the development of further knowledge and understanding.

Documentation

The recording and display of children's conversations, constructions, and other representations of their experiences derived from daily activities and special events serve the purpose of communicating (to parents, children, and the community at large) the children's experiences, their current understanding, how they think and reason, and where their interests lie. Documentation panels, which are usually created by the educator, are composed of photographs of events and objects children have created (e.g., three-dimensional objects, paintings) and are usually accompanied by recorded transcripts of children's conversations. Our goal in writing this section about documentation was to illustrate the importance of documentation as a communication tool, a record-keeping device, a source of information regarding changes in learning and understanding over time, and a means for helping children reflect on their previous experiences so they can decide what they would like to do next or learn more about. To this end, we included strategies for creating documentation panels in early childhood settings. As well, we designed some exercises that encouraged you to begin documenting and designing documentation panels. As an interesting addition, we introduced the idea of documenting your own learning process through the creation of a personal portfolio. This would allow you to record a history of your own journey through constructivism and provide you with a record of your own growth and development of practices that reflect a constructivist framework.

Reflection

A journey through the constructivist landscape *should not have an end* as constructivism is a theory about learning and as long as you are alive you should be in a situation where you continue to learn. As an educator, each year you welcome a new group of children into your class and because of this your classroom experiences should be different. Our purpose in encouraging you to engage in reflection is to enable you to be a flexible thinker, who is responsive to the needs and interests of each new group of children. To this end we have suggested that you reflect upon your understanding of the children's behaviours and the appropriate design and implementation of meaningful curriculum strategies with each unique group of children. We hope that the exercise we have recommended in the section on reflection has helped you engage in a meaningful form of reflection and that it has given you further insight into your classroom practices and helped you see where changes should be made.

We have come to the end of our journey together and while we will part ways with you at this point, we hope that you will continue along the constructivist route. It is important to remember that constructivism is a theory about learning, not a description of teaching. We wish you well as you continue learning about children, curriculum, and yourself as an educator.

Bibliography

Bloom, P.J., Sheerer, M., & Britz, J. (1991). *Blueprint for action: Achieving center-based change through staff development.* USA: New Horizons.

Carter, M. (1993). Catching teachers being good: Using observations to communicate. In E. Jones (Ed.), *Growing teachers: Partnership in staff development.* Washington DC: NAEYC.

Curtis, D., & Carter, M. (2000). *The art of awareness: How observation can transform your teaching.* St. Paul, MN: Redleaf Press.

Curtis, D., & Carter, M. (1996). *Reflecting children's lives: A handbook for planning child centered curriculum.* St. Paul, MN: Redleaf Press.

Epstein, A. (1993). *Training for quality: Improving early childhood programs through systematic inservice training.* Michigan: High/Scope Press.

Gandini, L., & Pope Edwards, C. (2001). *Bambini: The Italian approach to infant toddler care.* NY: Teacher's College Press.

Glickman, C.D., & Aldridge, D.P. (2001). Going public: The imperative of public education in the 31st century. In A Lieberman & L .Miller (Eds.), *Educators caught in the action: Professional development that matters.* (pp. 12-22). NY: Educators College Press.

Johnson, J., Christie, J., & Yawkey, T. (1999). *Play and early childhood development.* NY: Longman.

Marlowe, B.A., & Page, M.L. (1998). *Creating and sustaining the constructivist classroom.* Thousand Oaks, California: Corwin Press.

Reggio Children. (2001). *Making learning visible – Children as individual and group learners.* Reggio Emilia, Italy: Reggio Children.

Sobel, D. (1994). Authentic curriculum. *Holistic Education Review, 7,* 33-43.

Twomey-Fosnot, C. (2005). *Constructivism: Theory, perspectives and practice.* NY: Teachers College Press.